Trading Walls for Altars

Lindsay Allen

C2 Publishing/Mobile

For Jackson, Meredith, Sawyer, Elizabeth, and Marshall:
*"Come and hear, all you who fear God,
and I will tell what he has done for my soul."*
Psalm 66:16
May you soon have your own amazing stories to tell of God's
abounding love and faithfulness, but until then, you can enjoy mine.

For Derek:
"This is the LORD's doing; it is marvelous in our eyes."
Psalm 118:23
God has been so faithful to us, and I am forever grateful that He
chose to place us together to experience His amazing works
alongside one another.

Printed in the United States of America
ISBN 979-8-218-05118-1

NELLALLEN INC
6508 Sugar Creek Drive South
Mobile, AL 36695

www.thec2life.org

Contents

Recognizing Walls That Have Been There All Along

I grew up in the land of "Bless your heart! Hey y'all. Come on in. How y'all doin'? Fine, how 'bout you? Give me a neck hug. Stay a while. Y'all come back real soon, ya hear!" As a child, my family moved frequently from one southern town to another. Thankfully, I was pretty outgoing, so I easily started new friendships over the years which were mostly centered around common interests or activities. As a middle schooler, it was fairly easy to share my deepest thoughts and secrets with my besties (and keep theirs, too). However, when I entered adulthood, I never seemed to be able to break past the shallow pleasantries when trying to develop friendships. I was often shocked when marriages around me ended or when people within our church were found to be in scandal. I had no idea they were dealing with those serious things all along. These people had been carrying on as usual Sunday-in and Sunday-out, all while wearing smiles and smudge-free makeup.

I married my husband, Derek, when I was nineteen and instantly became a pastor's wife. This wasn't a shock to me like it is to a lot of women who marry someone in vocational ministry. In fact, I grew up as a pastor's kid, and I felt strongly from a young age that I would marry someone in ministry. As a pastor's wife, people kept me at a safe distance from their real struggles and problems. They wanted to be liked by me and to sit by me, but they didn't want to be known by me. I had my part to play in staying in the shallows as well. I had heard from countless other pastors' wives that you can't make friends with the people you serve. It's not safe. You'll be hurt, or worse, you'll hurt your and your husband's ministry. That advice combined with my perspective as a pastor's kid witnessing several church people act a fool, it seemed to just make sense. Authenticity just wasn't going to happen for me outside of my marriage. The first real adult friendships I formed were with Derek's best friend, Randy and his wife, Rachel. Even with them it took us years to get to a place of openness with one another where we felt the freedom to share real struggles. All the more, much of our comfort with one another was built on the years of friendship

Derek and Randy had already developed with each other beginning their kindergarten year. For years I was envious of their friendship. I remember thinking, "I will never have a real friend like that because I can't go back to kindergarten and build one."

My world changed in 2013 when my husband and I, along with our three kids at the time, moved from north Alabama to Miami, Florida, to plant a church. We quickly learned that people in South Florida were night-and-day different from those we had known in the cultural south. Things worked differently there. No one trusted anyone. People were overly suspicious and seemed to be just waiting for some catch or for the other shoe to drop at any moment. People generally expected that others only wanted something from them, or more specifically, to take advantage of them in some way. Our first realization of these nuances occurred when we tried to rent a house in Miami before actually arriving in the city. It was an impossible task! We were working with a real estate agent who tried unsuccessfully to get us into several rental contracts. She explained to us that none of the landlords would agree to rent to us until we were actually there in Miami. They didn't believe we were credible, potential tenants. Instead, they suspected it was some kind of a scam. So, praying for God to provide, we loaded up our U-Haul and just drove south. Our agent called us about half-way through the drive down and said, "I just left your house! The landlords don't know that it's your house yet, but it meets all your requests and (most importantly) your budget. They want to meet you tomorrow before agreeing to lease you the house. I need you to go in there, put on that southern charm, and bring your baby!" That's just what we did. Sure enough, they agreed to lease us the house despite the three other prospective tenants who were touring the home during our meeting. This helped us learn that our baby, along with our other two kids, was a fantastic tool to break the ice with new people. The would-be cold-shouldered people would let a little of their guard down around our kids and actually engage in conversation with them and, consequently, us. This was a huge win for us when we were trying to meet and gather people.

Soon after moving to Miami, we planned our first prayer meeting. We had met a few people during visits to the city before moving, so we contacted everyone we knew (all twelve of them) and invited them to our home to help us pray for the new church we were starting and other specific prayer needs. At first, it didn't appear that anyone was going to show up. But, in true Miami fashion, about ten minutes after our announced start time, people started ringing the doorbell. Pretty soon, our living room was full of new faces. We took some time for introductions since no one knew each other before gathering that night. After the introductions, we gave instructions for the structured time of prayer. We set up stations around our living room with prayer prompts and Scripture to guide people's prayer time. It was all going so well! Then, we decided to finish the night by giving the group an opportunity to share their own prayer requests. Now, where I grew up, this would be the time when people would start asking for prayer for their uncle's neighbor's dog's left paw infection. So, you can imagine my shock when people started sharing real needs, like "Pray for me to be better about reading the Bible," or "Pray for me to have more healthy relationships." Then, I was really floored when it came time for the young couple in the circle to share. The husband went first. He shared with us his struggle with viewing pornography and asked us to pray for him and his wife and their baby girl to be able to have victory over the effects of his temptation and sin. I felt my face get flushed and all I could think was "What, what did he just say? His wife is sitting *right there*! What was his name again?" It felt like we were playing the what's in your purse game, and he had brought his Mary Poppins magic duffle bag. He just kept bringing out things that neither Derek nor I expected could come from such little investment in his life. The two opposite cultures represent extremes on a scale of emotional connectivity. Understanding where we and others fall on that scale has helped me better relate to and connect with others. In addition, it highlighted some unhealthy truths about my own life that needed to be addressed.

Part 1: Learning the Lingo

We All Have Walls

"Her heart was a secret garden and the walls were very high."
—William Goldman, The Princess Bride[1]

The Highs and Lows

Both my culture of origin and the culture I found myself among in Miami led me to realize that people have two distinct emotional layers. At times, I've heard them described as walls. These two walls serve as barriers to the genuine person deep inside. The first wall is a person's exterior wall. This wall is the first one you encounter when meeting or getting to know them. It's a big part of that first impression, but also the impression they desire for you to have about them, even in a long-term relationship. The second wall is the interior wall. This wall is the one guarding who they really are inside. This wall is holding back all the deepest, most intimate parts of the person. If you breach that wall, you're in. Really in. Everyone has these two walls, but not all walls are created equal.

In a typical person from the cultural south, their outside wall is very low, even cute. You can just step right over it with a happy hop. A good southern belle or gent will open a door for you and look you in the eye and say, "Good morning." They will smile and let you go before them, and they will stop to help you if you are in a tough spot. They'll bring you a casserole when you're sick, and they will chat your ears off

---

[1] Goldman, *The Princess Bride.*

about their interests or kids/grandkids. But don't be fooled. Behind that "bless your heart" is a passive aggressive mumbler who can't believe you would even attempt to successfully bake their famous sweet potato casserole for the potluck dinner. Their adorable little exterior wall is tucked neatly in front of their mammoth inside wall that could rival the security level of Fort Knox. Want to know what keeps them awake at night? Want to know what they battle with on the weekends? Want to know what they can't stop watching, listening to, or thinking about? Want to know their deepest fears and doubts? Well, invest a good ten years, and maybe they'll slip up and let you know one day by accident. You're going to need a team of professionals with blueprints, heavy artillery, high-tech gadgets, and SEAL training to get past that wall.

In Miami, the outside wall for most people is tall, smooth, and sleek, so there is no chance of getting a foothold to climb it. It's pretty. A lot of money has been invested to make it look appealing, and it's painted with beautiful, bright colors that pop. Careful, though, because at the top, if by some chance you make it there, is razor wire. No one is going to let you merge into their lane of traffic. For that matter, if they even see a blinker working on your car, they will speed up and cut you off just to make you work as hard for a spot as they did! They won't look you in the eye on the Metro. And don't expect the cashier to say hello back to you in the drive through (it became a game for my husband and me to see how many times we could say it and how loud we would have to become before we would finally be acknowledged . . . if ever). That outside wall is almost impossible to penetrate, but if you do, you'll find the inner wall is as short as a cup of Cuban *Cafecito*. You'll become part of their family knowing every (many times shocking) detail of their lives, many of which would make any southern girl blush. You'll be kissed on the cheek with every greeting and go through the multi-layered goodbye process every time you part. You'll be invited to family Christmas and have people in your home at all hours baring their souls.

It's Not an Exact Science

Now, you might be reading this and thinking, "I don't match those descriptions," and that is very possible. It's helpful to think of it like a spectrum. Generally speaking, most culturally southern people have low exterior walls and high interior walls, but there are plenty of southern people with the reverse, or even high exterior *and* interior walls for that matter. The same is true for some Miamians. Even the classification of "low" and "high" could be varying levels from person to person. Some people with very high exterior walls might come across as quiet, behind-the-scenes, or even shy. They are the kind of person of whom you might say, "Once you get to know them, they become a different person!" Oftentimes, fears, life experiences, and insecurities have led them to build tall exterior walls to keep people at what feels to be a safe distance. In contrast, many people with very high interior walls can be the most successful at gathering others. They are always meeting new people and can often be seen as the life of the party, but they can't seem to keep friendships for long periods of time with the same people. Their friendships never dive deeper than the small talk and party games.

Why Walls?

So, what's our fascination with walls? Let's take the modern world's most famous wall, for example. The Great Wall of China was constructed over a period of about 2,000 years, costing over a million human lives and over $42 billion. Stretching over 5,500 feet long, it never actually prevented even one invasion. Even the old adage that it's visible from space isn't true. Although the wall is plenty long enough, it is way too thin to be seen by the naked eye even from a low-earth orbit according to NASA[2]. Its biggest success has been as a tourist trap or wallpaper image. What a parable for our emotional walls. They protect until they don't. They seem like a good idea, but they are never really enough. We think we are going to protect what's inside, but just like with the Chinese, it's the lives inside that die building it while the enemy outside just walks on in like Genghis Khan.

---

[2] See britanica.com and nasa.gov

Now consider the Belfast Peace Walls. These walls were built in Ireland in the late 1960s in order to keep the Irish Catholics separated from the Irish Protestants with the hopes of maintaining peace. Instead, the walls highlighted the differences among the groups and caused the people to feel abnormally segmented from their neighbors. Real peace comes not from hiding behind barriers separating us from those who are different from us, rather it comes when we are able to share common space despite our opposing views. It's like saying that the best way to teach my kids how to be at peace with one another is to give them each their own rooms. They will not learn how to live peacefully simply by being separated. They may learn how to find a peaceful place, but not how to *be* at peace. The moment one of them enters the other's room or a common living space, that peace quickly vanishes if the individuals have not learned the art of making and keeping peace. If we are seeking to be at peace with those around us, the answer is not to build thicker, taller, stronger walls. Peace requires real listening, real sharing, real repentance, real forgiveness, real crying, real laughing, and good food helps. Sharing time around a meal can be a wonderful avenue toward peace with a brother or sister.

Of course, who can forget the Bible's most famous wall, the wall of Jericho? This was the wall standing between God's chosen people and the land God had promised to give them. The people of Jericho were counting on their wall to be enough to keep anyone or anything threatening out. Maybe you'll remember the story according to Veggie Tales[3]. Those soldier peas were beaming with pride as they sang, "Keep walking, but you won't knock down our wall! Keep walking, but she isn't going to fall!" I'm sure there really was a level of pride that came with having such a fortified wall protecting them (the real people of Jericho, that is, not the vegetable version). Isn't that like us? Don't we take pride in our illusion of perfection and control? When we manage to fool people enough to think we have it all, or maybe just enough of it, together, we can begin to believe we actually do. Friends, that is the anti-Gospel. We can't possibly come close to having it all or even just a little of it together. Every fiber of our being has been touched and cursed by sin, and anything that is together in us has been mended by a loving Savior and sealed by the beloved Holy Spirit. It's like a pretty privacy fence. It might look nice from the road, but

---

[3] *Veggie Tales: Josh and the Big Wall, 1997*

chances are, the backyard is a mess! There's junk back there that hasn't been dealt with in years. You've just given up and started weed eating around it every once in a while. Jesus used the word picture of white-washed tombs. At first glance it's appealing to the eye, but inside it looks and smells like death itself.

The Walls Closest to Home

We all have walls. Some of us have walls that were carefully and strategically placed over what seems like millennia, only to malfunction when a real enemy launched an attack. We built that thin but lengthy wall year after year, fear after fear, rejection after rejection, failure after failure, embarrassment after embarrassment, comparison after comparison. It cost us greatly, but we didn't win. Some of us have walls that went up in hopes of making or keeping peace, but peace has not been found, and now we just feel strangely separated and alone. Some of us have walls that were built to be a facade and illusion to fool those on the outside looking in, but the paint is starting to chip and the cracks are showing through. Some of us have walls that were quickly fortified when we slammed the doors shut at the sight of danger. Maybe it was a tragedy or an abuse that instantly slammed that wall door for you, and when it did, you turned the deadbolt and set the alarm to "stay." But, just like Jericho, one loud blast can allow the opposing army to walk right in on us. If the walls are bound to crumble anyway, why continue building them? Why not build something that matters?

What if we used the materials from crumbled or deconstructed walls to build altars instead? What if we worked to push against division and isolation and pressed into real relationships, first with God and then by extension with others. My hope for readers of this book is that you will learn how to identify the walls in your life keeping you from real, life-giving relationships and recognize opportunities to trade those walls for altars. Each chapter will end with a few questions for reflection. I encourage you, at the very least, to put some serious thought into your answers. Even better, write your answers in a journal, or better still, discuss the chapter and your answers with your spouse, a friend, or a group of friends that you desire to become more intimately connected with. These questions are not well suited for a casual or large group discussion since they promote vulnerability and might disclose some raw truth.

Questions for Reflection

1. What's the largest wall you've ever seen in person? Maybe it was the side of a skyscraper or a long sea wall that stretched for miles. How did you feel when you got close to it? Did it make you feel small? Safe? Dizzy?

2. On a scale from 1 (a cute little step-sized wall) to 10 (the top reaches the giant's house in the clouds) how tall is your outside wall? Has it always been that size? What events do you think led you to build that wall?

3. Now, using that same scale, how would you describe the size of your inside wall? What events do you think led you to build that wall? Who are the people who have cracked that wall and have really been given access to who you are?

2

Altars Can Be Messy

"Our vision is so limited we can hardly imagine a love that does not show itself in protection from suffering. The love of God is of a different nature altogether. It does not hate tragedy. It never denies reality. It stands in the very teeth of suffering."
—Elisabeth Elliot[4]

Where Did Altars Come From?

The first mention we find in Scripture of an altar being built is in Genesis 8 after God remembered Noah, his family, and the animals by protecting them from the worldwide flood through their journey on the ark. After spending a year cooped up inside a ship with literally every kind of animal in existence, the doors finally opened, and the land was wide open for Noah and his family. What was the first thing on Noah's post-quarantine to-do list? It wasn't eating out, going for a run, or building a new and improved home. No, Scripture records that the first thing Noah did after exiting the ark was build an altar to the Lord. Why? Why would he choose to do this first? Well, something significant had just happened, actually a few somethings significant. The first significant thing was that God had just spared him and his family from death and destruction when no one else on the planet was spared. I would imagine that could bring about a sense of gratitude to a

---

[4] Elliot, *Passion and Purity*.

guy. Secondly, but even more significant, is that the God of heaven verbally spoke to Noah. The verses just before the account of Noah's altar building tell us that God spoke to Noah and said, "Go out from the ark, you and your wife, and your sons and your sons' wives with you. Bring out with you every living thing that is with you of all flesh—birds and animals and every creeping thing that creeps on the earth—that they may swarm on the earth, and be fruitful and multiply on the earth." It is immediately followed by the words "So Noah went out, and his sons and his wife and his sons' wives with him. Every beast, every creeping thing, and every bird, everything that moves on the earth, went out by families from the ark."[5] Immediate and simple obedience to the Lord by Noah literally led to the salvation of his life and his family's lives. That pattern of obedience continued in his disemb*ark*ing (pun intended). Noah had an encounter with God. God greatly impacted Noah's life in such a way that his life could never be the same. He took time and used whatever resources were available to him in that moment to stop and commemorate the amazing work God had done. He didn't want to just walk off the boat and move along like everything that just happened was normal and insignificant.

I guess you could say altar building really took off at that point, because after that, altars were built all throughout the Bible. The pattern for altar building went like this: God spoke -> hearer obeyed -> obedience led to life change -> altar was built. Overwhelmingly, people built altars in order to show gratitude to God for His work in their lives at that particular moment and to commemorate that specific encounter with God. Sometimes an altar was built before the events fully unfolded as a demonstration of trust that those things God spoke would, in fact, come to pass. This was the case with Abraham's altar built in Genesis 12 in response to God's promise to give the land to his offspring, which at the time numbered . . . zero people. Isaac built an altar in Genesis 26 when God reiterated to him the promises that were originally given to his father, Abraham. Other times an altar was built after events happened in order to reflect on what God had already done, as was the case for the altar built by Jacob in Genesis 35 when God reminded him of His recent protection over him when he escaped from his brother, Esau's pursuits. David built an altar in 1 Chronicles 21 when he realized his sin as a leader and its effect on those whom he was responsible to lead. He knew that only God could save them, and

---

[5] Genesis 8:15-19

He was full of mercy unlike any other. David's altar was a cry to the Lord for mercy, and thank God, He answered. Joshua built an altar in Joshua 22 when the Lord miraculously brought the Israelites through the Jordan River. This altar is particularly interesting because Scripture tells us they wanted to commemorate that miracle moment not just for those present that day, but also for future generations who would see it there as they passed by. Gideon built an altar in Judges 6 when war was raging around him and defeat seemed certain, yet the Lord spoke and delivered peace to him. He wanted to specifically remember the peace he found in the Lord that day, so up went the altar.

We Have the Wood for the Altar, but Where Is the Sacrifice?

While we recognize that altars served as ways to memorialize a person's encounter and relationship with God, we can't look past the how. How did an altar consecrate a person to the Lord? It provided a location set apart specifically for the offering of a sacrifice. Sometimes the sacrifice was a grain offering or incense offering, but most of the time the sacrifice required a blood offering. God established this system Himself from the very beginning when, in Genesis 3, Adam and Eve invited sin into creation. Their sin had opened their eyes to their nakedness and brought a new emotion of shame into their hearts. They knew they were naked, and they had the bright idea to just cover it up themselves by making some floppy fig leaf apparel. About the time they had finished tailoring their new outfits, God showed up on the scene to confront their sin. But, being a loving and merciful God, He chose not to leave them in the inadequate and, by this point, likely itchy clothing. He killed some animals to create appropriate and suitable clothing for them. See the message God was stating? Where there is sin, there must be a blood sacrifice to cover it. This message continued throughout the Old Testament with the sacrificial system and reached a pinnacle in Genesis 22. Abraham had been promised by God to be the father of a great nation. This nation would come through his offspring with Sarah. The problem was that he and Sarah didn't have any offspring, and they were both well beyond childbearing years. However, God revealed Himself to be the One in control of opening and closing the womb, and He fulfilled His promise to Abraham by giving them a son, Isaac. When Isaac was twelve years old, God asked Abraham to bring him up the mountain and offer him as a sacrifice. Abraham obeyed immediately! This was not the same Abraham who lied about his wife twice to save his own skin earlier in the book of Genesis⁶. He had grown in faith so much since then that he was now willing to take his son up a mountain to build an altar with no backup plan for a sacrifice. He was confident they would both return somehow. He trusted that God was able to raise Isaac from the dead if He needed to. He knew for certain that God would fulfill His end of the bargain with Abraham, and He would do it through Isaac, because that is what He said He would do. On that mountain, God provided a blood sacrifice and did not require Abraham to give up his beloved son.

Then, generations later, on a similar (if not the same) mountain, God Himself gave up His beloved Son so that everyone who believes in Him could have forgiveness and eternal life. That altar was the most beautiful but the ugliest all at the same time. The altar was made of rugged wood in the shape of a cross and the Sacrifice on it was Jesus, the spotless Lamb who came to take away the sins of the world. The weight the altar held was heavy. It held the sin of the entire world past, present and future. There had been an encounter with God, all right. God had become a man and lived a sinless life among sinful people. He healed. He taught. He warned. He loved. He cared. As a result, there was life change for countless people both in that moment and for generations yet to be numbered. Even today, the image of that particular altar holds infinite meaning for people all over the world. People wear it, decorate with it, and place it at the tops of places of worship as a sign of hope for all who see it. When we see a cross, it often serves to draw our minds and hearts to the work of Jesus. This is what an altar is all about. It serves as a tangible reminder of the work of God in our lives and directs our focus toward Him.

What Does This Mean for Me?

The altar of the cross was full of suffering, as most altars are. This is why God set up the sacrificial system in the first place, long before Jesus ever walked the earth. He wanted to point toward Jesus and the cross for generations before He ever came, so that when He did come it would fit perfectly, like the missing piece of a puzzle. Jesus was Who it had been all about all along. Now, we go to altars to look

---

⁶ Genesis 12 and 20

back on what Jesus has already done. We no longer have to bring a guilt offering in order to be in right standing with God. No more priest tying a rope around his waist and bells on his shoes in case of sudden death when entering the presence of God in the Holy of Holies. Jesus paid in full the guilt offering for us with His death on the cross. He offers us forgiveness, communion with God, and eternal life if we confess our sin to Him and believe that God raised Him from the dead. When we choose to follow Jesus, we choose a life of dying to ourselves.

Following Jesus means our life is no longer our own, and that's a good thing! He's the King of life. He created it! As my husband often puts it, "Jesus is so good at life that He never attended a funeral that He didn't ruin by raising the person from the dead . . . including His own." So, if Jesus knows life better than we do, why not let Him be in charge of ours, too? If we are going to allow Jesus to be the Author and Perfecter of our life, we are going to need to demolish some walls. No more secret gardens allowed. But good news! That will leave some great raw materials lying around for us to use to build some beautiful altars to the Lord.

Questions for Reflection

1. Which biblical altar mentioned in this chapter resonated the most with you in the current season of your life and why?
2. When was a time in your life that you just "walked off the boat" and moved along to the next normal thing? In other words, when did God intervene on your behalf, and instead of stopping to acknowledge Him in a special way, you just carried on with life as usual?
3. On a scale of 1 (my life is mine and He can't have it . . . my Precious) to 10 (My life is His, and I've surrendered every thought, relationship, plan, dream, dollar and cent to His care) where would you place yourself today in your level of surrender to Jesus Christ?

3

Do the Hard Things

"Courage, dear heart."
—C. S. Lewis, *The Voyage of the Dawn Treader*[7]

Demolition

How do we actually make the trade from walls to altars? How do we tear down the walls that keep us tucked in tightly, only then to use those broken pieces to build meaningful altars? What tools do we really have, and how effective are they against the brick and mortar of our emotions and experiences? How does the remaining rubble become something worthy of holding an offering to the Lord? Well, my opinions and best tips are powerless, but the Word of God is full of power and wisdom, and it speaks to this directly. Let's see what it has to say.

In 2 Corinthians 12:9-10, Paul shares, "But he [the Lord] said to me, 'My grace is sufficient for you, for my power is made perfect in weakness.' Therefore I will boast all the more gladly of my weaknesses, so that the power of Christ may rest upon me. For the sake of Christ, then, I am content with weaknesses, insults, hardships, persecutions, and calamities. For when I am weak, then I am strong." Do you see God's formula for our strength? His grace applied to our weakness equals our strength through the perfection of His power. God, through

---

[7] Lewis, *The Voyage of the Dawn Treader.*

the apostle Paul, explains to us that when we are weak it becomes an opportunity for God Himself to do an incredible and powerful work in our lives that will strengthen us rather than break us. This passage is not an example of the kind of boasting that points to Paul. It's not like he is fishing for compliments, as we often do. He's not saying these things just so people will say, "Oh, Paul, you're not really all that bad! You are actually really strong!" No, that motive would only falsely prop up his ego, or as we more commonly describe it, build his self-esteem. Paul was not looking to esteem himself with his boasting. Quite the opposite, Paul brought glory to God when, in his weakness, Christ's power rested on him. The list of scenarios that Paul would boast in are not lightweight. Sure, the first few are fairly low level . . . weaknesses, insults, hardships. Then things get super serious with persecutions and calamities. We are talking about life-altering events that should wreck a person. Instead, through the power of Christ, strength can be found! The first step in the demolition is to bring our weaknesses to Christ and to receive His power that will rest on us when we trust and follow Him. We must see every hurt, every insufficiency, every betrayal, and every failure as an opportunity to boast in the work of Christ. If we think of those things as building materials, we then have a choice. With it we can either choose to build a wall, or an altar. For many of us, we have chosen over and over to stack them in the shape of walls.

So, what tools do we have to break down the walls that have already been built? Scripture gives us four tools to deconstruct any standing walls that we have used to push others away.

1. Repent wholeheartedly.
"If they repent with all their heart and with all their soul in the land of their enemies, who carried them captive, and pray to you toward their land, which you gave to their fathers, the city that you have chosen, and the house that I have built for your name, then hear in heaven your dwelling place their prayer and their plea, and maintain their cause and forgive your people who have sinned against you, and all their transgressions that they have committed against you, and grant them compassion in the sight of those who carried them captive, that they may have compassion on them." 1 Kings 8:48-50

Certainly, the command to repent is very present in both the Old and New Testaments, but this passage stood out to me with its answer to the question, "How much?" We are to repent with all our heart and soul. This is not "I'm sorry *if* I hurt you," or "I'm sorry, *but* . . ." This is "I am sorry. Will you forgive me?" We repent to God because He is the One whom we have sinned against. Remember David's big sin? The time he stole another man's wife and then had said man sent to the hardest part of the battle to ensure his death? When David was convicted of his sin, he confessed and repented to God saying, "Against you, and you only, have I sinned." He recognized God as the Lawgiver, and when he broke that law, his transgression was against the Lawgiver Himself. When we repent to God, He freely forgives us. Once we are forgiven and see our sin the way God sees it, we cannot help but also see how our sin has affected other people. Consequently, when we see the effects our sin has on others, we should desire to seek forgiveness from them as well, in order to reconcile that relationship that was broken. Matthew 3:8 puts it this way, "Bear fruit in keeping with repentance." It is a sign of growth, health, and life when we repent to our fellow man.

2. Forgive tenderly.

"Let no corrupting talk come out of your mouths, but only such as is good for building up, as fits the occasion, that it may give grace to those who hear. And do not grieve the Holy Spirit of God, by whom you were sealed for the day of redemption. Let all bitterness and wrath and anger and clamor and slander be put away from you, along with all malice. Be kind to one another, tenderhearted, forgiving one another, as God in Christ forgave you." Ephesians 4:29-32

In the instances that our walls have been built by the sin of others against us, we have to remove those toxic bricks of bitterness, wrath, anger, clamor, slander, and malice. These blocks are too easily stacked when we are the victim. They are just so close and easily within our reach. They fit so perfectly in our hands, and they balance so well on one another, almost magnetically. Rejecting our natural desire to build walls with these corrupt characteristics paves the way for us to give grace to those around us. How? We show grace to others by being kind, tenderhearted, and forgiving. Why? We forgive others not because they have earned our forgiveness. We forgive others not because they deserve to be forgiven. We forgive others not because they have asked for it properly and in a timely manner. We forgive others because God in Christ has forgiven us. Romans 5:8 reminds us that "While we were still sinners, Christ died for us." That's tender forgiveness

3. Serve humbly.

"So if there is any encouragement in Christ, any comfort from love, any participation in the Spirit, any affection and sympathy, complete my joy by being of the same mind, having the same love, being in full accord and of one mind. Do nothing from selfish ambition or conceit, but in humility count others more significant than yourselves. Let each of you look not only to his own interests, but also to the interests of others. Have this mind among yourselves, which is yours in Christ Jesus, who, though he was in the form of God, did not count equality with God a thing to be grasped, but emptied himself, by taking the form of a servant, being born in the likeness of men. And being found in human form, he humbled himself by becoming obedient to the point of death, even death on a cross. Therefore, God has highly exalted him and bestowed on him the name that is above every name, so that at the name of Jesus every knee should bow, in heaven and on earth and under the earth, and every tongue confess that Jesus Christ is Lord, to the glory of God the Father." Philippians 2:1-11

Once we have been forgiven through our confession and repentance, and we have forgiven others through the extension of grace from the Holy Spirit within us, then what? Where do we go from there? Scripture is clear here. We serve! It is one thing to say to someone, "I forgive you." It is a totally different thing to serve that person and even give up your life for them. This was the model Christ gave to us. He left perfection and His throne in heaven to come and take on the likeness of man. He humbled himself to serve and die a criminal's death so that we could experience eternal life. There is no offense someone could commit toward us greater than our offense toward Christ, yet He came. He served. He died. We are called to empty ourselves and think greater of the interests of others, counting other people as more significant than ourselves. This feels impossible, but Jesus is not commanding us to do anything He wasn't willing to do Himself. He is also not asking us to do this in our own strength and power. We can do this through the "encouragement of Christ" and the "participation in the Spirit." He is with us and will help us serve those around us who are most difficult to serve. When we serve others, it sends waves of love and joy crashing into the walls that guard our hearts and theirs. The erosion of those walls brings comfort, affection, and sympathy both to us and to those we serve.

4. Repeat frequently.

"Then Peter came to him and said, 'Lord, how many times could my brother sin against me and I forgive him? As many as seven times?' 'I tell you, not as many as seven,' Jesus said to him, 'but seventy times seven.'" Matthew 18:21-22

This is the kicker. It seems pretty easy to repent of "that one time I messed up" or to forgive "that person who did that thing that time," or to serve "now that everything is right between us," but it is a totally different thickness of wall when it is an ongoing struggle. What does Jesus say about habits, multiple failures, and ongoing struggles? He says, "Again. Do it again." This passage is not intended to tell us that there is an exact number of instances that a person has until they can no longer be forgiven for a particular sin. In the Bible, the number seven represents completion. Jesus is telling Peter that he should forgive others repeatedly and completely (specifically, completely times completely in the tens place) as many times as they repent. Because we continue to live with our own sinful nature among people with their own sinful natures, we continue to revisit issues, repent, forgive, and serve. Completely.

Reconstruction

Sometimes the walls come down with one loud blast like the walls of Jericho, and other times they come down brick by brick, section by section, over years and even decades, like the Berlin Wall. Once the walls are finally down, we, like Noah, have the opportunity to rebuild something greater than what was lost. Acts 3:19-20 says, "Repent therefore, and turn back, that your sins may be blotted out, that times of refreshing may come from the presence of the Lord." We have the invitation to experience times of refreshing in God's presence! God invites us to spend time with Him. How do we do that? We worship. When we spend time with God, it's called worship. Altars are specific places made for worship. We have the privilege to worship God on the altars of our hearts and not just in the pews (or chairs) of our churches.

We can build altars in our hearts by investing precious time in private and public worship of God. Paul encourages us in Romans 12:1-2, "I appeal to you therefore, brothers, by the mercies of God, to present your bodies as a living sacrifice, holy and acceptable to God, which is your spiritual worship. Do not be conformed to this world, but be transformed by the renewal of your mind, that by testing you may discern what is the will of God, what is good and acceptable and perfect." Worship involves the renewal of our mind. In the same way that we cannot eat endless loaves of homemade sourdough bread and cake pops without consequence to our midsection, we also cannot feed our minds junk food, empty deceit, and philosophies of this world and expect to have healthy souls. It's a simple matter of intake and output. Our minds can be renewed by time spent in God's Word, and according to Scripture, that leads to our transformation.

When transformation happens, we should commemorate it and even celebrate it. When God does a great work in your life or brings you through a difficult season, don't just move on with business as usual. Stop and worship. Build an altar in your heart by having a special moment of worship with the Lord, remembering His goodness. Bring Him your weaknesses and raw materials. You will be amazed at what He can do with them. Find a Scripture passage, verse, or maybe even a word that represents that special moment or season with God, and write it on your heart. Then, write it in a journal, or on some artwork, or on your mirror, or like a friend of mine does, on your arm with temporary tattoo ink. Let them serve as reminders for yourself so that when you see them your heart is reminded of all God has done. Let them also serve as conversation starters with family, friends, and passersby. Use them to tell of God's amazing work in your life. This is a pleasing aroma to the Lord. This is a beautiful offering to Him. Saturating your life with God's Word is not an easy task. It takes much effort and often means choosing not to do other enjoyable or even good things. The benefits, however, far outweigh the cost. It requires great courage to do the hard things like repent, forgive, serve, and worship. Courage, dear heart.

Questions for Reflection

1. What is one weakness you have that needs an application of God's grace?
2. Which of the four tools of deconstruction is the most difficult for you? Why?
3. What is one way this week you can surround yourself more with God's Word?

Part 2: Making the Trade

Trading a Storybook Character for a Savior

"We ought to live as if Jesus died yesterday, rose this morning, and is coming back this afternoon."
—Adrian Rogers[8]

From My Story

I've been attending church since nine months before I was born. Each week I sat in a Sunday School class on Sunday morning, discipleship training on Sunday night, and GAs on Wednesday night. In other words, I was at church any and every time the doors were open. Many of those lessons were taught using stories from *The Bible Storybooks'* watercolor illustrated set of encyclopedias or using felt characters and accessories on a large green wrinkled felt board. I knew the plot and events of most of the big stories from the Bible, similarly to how I knew Mother Goose rhymes and "The Three Little Pigs." Jesus was a cool character in sensational stories that captured my imagination. I knew about Him, but I didn't know Him. By the young age of six, I had built a wall made of knowledge and familiarity of the story character, Jesus, around my heart. Yes, I knew the answers to the comprehension questions at the end of the lesson. If the teacher's hand

---

cramped up and she needed someone to come rearrange the felt pieces for the next scene, I could handle it.

Unbeknownst to me, this wall was shielding the deepest parts of my little heart, keeping me from recognizing my own sin and knowing the most important Person ever. Jesus Himself, through the work of the Holy Spirit, knew just how to get through that weak little wall to speak directly to my soul and introduce Himself to me. I suddenly felt the weight of my own sin as best a six-year-old can, and I knew it wasn't enough for me to know the stories. I knew with my soul and not just my mind that my sin was real, and the Bible was telling me that the wages of my sin was death. God used the lyrics in the song "I Have Decided to Follow Jesus" to awaken my soul to my need for salvation. I needed to be forgiven and free, not entertained and enthralled. A storybook character wasn't going to cut it here. I needed a Savior.

So, I made the trade. I tore down that wall that I had been hiding behind. The wall was built of "I know that Bible story, so I'm ok!" and of "I go to church every time the doors are open," and even of "my dad is the pastor, so I must be good with God." With the fallen scraps of the downed wall, I built an altar of "I confess I am a sinner and I choose to follow Jesus anywhere and in any way He leads." The altar I built to commemorate God's saving work in my life looked like me walking down an aisle at a summer camp named "Camp Back 40," praying to receive Christ as my Savior, then publicly worshiping Him through baptism on August 19, 1989. The offering I had to give was myself, and the Lord sealed me with His promised Holy Spirit. After this first encounter with Jesus, my Savior, I have never been the same .

There are certain memories from that week at camp, and even my baptism day, that come to my mind frequently and cause me to worship the Lord all over again. Some of them are obvious, like I can't hear that old hymn without thinking of that moment of new beginning for me, or I can't see an old child-sized wooden straight back chair without thinking of the one I sat in to converse with the camp pastor about the Truth of the Gospel. Others are not as obvious, like New Kids on the Block merchandise. My sleeping bag for the camp was covered with NKOTB and, for some reason, that stuck in my mind. Also, snakes. The first time I ever saw a real snake in the wild was at that camp, and it freaked me out for sure! Who knows? Maybe seeing a snake, or as Bill Bubba Bussey calls it, the Devil's hand puppet, up close is what softened my heart to my need for the Gospel. I'll never forget when my mom gave me a box of memorabilia shortly after I got married, and in it was my baptism certificate. I didn't remember the date of my baptism before seeing that paper, and I was blown away when I learned the date was exactly, to the day, eleven years prior to my first date with Derek, and twelve years prior to the day he proposed to me. Those memories serve as building blocks of an altar on my heart that allow me to offer a sacrifice of thanksgiving to God over and over in my life for His saving work, and I visit that altar often.

From God's Story

There is a woman in Scripture who had heard stories of Jesus. She had a good idea of who the Messiah would be and what He would do, or so she thought. In John 4, we get a glimpse of this Samaritan woman who was such an outcast that she couldn't go to the "water cooler" at the same time as the rest of the girls. She went to the well during the hottest part of the day because it was easier. It was not physically easier. In fact, it was physically exhausting to have to carry such a heavy load at the hottest part of the day. No, it was easier because she didn't have to see the stares of the other women, hear their whispers about her, or pretend she didn't notice them shunning her. She had built a wall of isolation by avoiding the common spaces when she knew the other women would be there.

When Jesus first spoke to the woman, asking her to give Him a drink of water, she responded with a push back. She said, "'How is it that You, a Jew, ask for a drink from me, a Samaritan woman?' For Jews do not associate with Samaritans." Miss Samaritan felt Someone leaning on her outer wall which clearly had "keep out!" painted on it. She reminded Him of the social rules in hopes that He would back off of her outer wall. Instead, He gently carved a tunnel through that wall by telling her the hidden truth of her life like only God could do. Sure, she knew about Jacob and his descendants. She knew about places of worship and theological arguments. She even had some information about the coming Messiah. She knew that He was called "Christ" and that He would be able to explain things better once He came. None of this knowledge affected her life personally. She had the storybook character all worked out in her mind. Her walls caused her to literally sit right beside the Messiah Himself and not recognize Him.

Then, she encountered the Savior. Suddenly, nothing behind her wall of isolation was hidden anymore. Jesus cut straight to her need for His living water. He bypassed her facade she had set up to keep everyone out, and He connected with her soul. This interaction with Jesus caused the woman to drop her jar and run toward those she had avoided for so long. She had to tell the people whom she had likely avoided for years about the man who told her everything she ever did. The Messiah himself had come to her! He offered her parched soul lasting refreshment. What a difference a Savior makes. Our daily lives should point to the power of a Savior who died, rose, and will come again.

From Your Story

1. If you could go back in time, which story of Jesus would you choose to have witnessed firsthand? Why?
2. The woman at the well was forever changed by her interaction with Jesus as Savior. What is one thing that has changed about your life since you met Jesus?
3. What is one way you can/did build an altar to remember your encounter with Jesus as your Savior? Have you followed your salvation experience with public baptism? Have you written down your story of who you were before you met Jesus, how you met Jesus, and who you are now in Christ? If so, have you shared it with anyone lately?

5

Trading Stereotypes for Surrender

"God is always more concerned with the decision-maker than he is with the decision itself."
—Jen Wilkin[9]

From My Story

When I was a teenager, my church youth group annually attended a youth retreat that took place during the last days of December and went into the first days of January. They called it "Exit" followed by the year that we were exiting. At Exit '96, we did all the typical youth trip things Gatlinburg, Tennessee, could offer. In our free time we went to fun dinners including the one in the huge arena with animatronic Dolly Parton singing as we ate our oversized roasted chicken. Our itinerary also included ice skating, shopping, and of course, staring through the window to watch taffy being made. The majority of our time, however, was spent in worship services where hundreds of teens from dozens of churches had gathered from all over the southeast. The Exit retreat staff did include the always-entertaining talent show each year, but the main purpose was the worship. I was enjoying it all and sad when we approached the last day.

---

[9] Wilkin, *In His Image: 10 Ways God Calls Us to Reflect His Character.*

During the last evening service, the camp pastor, Paul, was closing things out with a time of invitation like he had at the conclusion of each previous service that week. This time went differently. As we were all singing, he interrupted the music to say, "I don't normally do things like this, but I feel strongly that the Lord is telling me that there is one young man here who needs to give his life to ministry and one young lady here who needs to give her life to missions." It was like someone hit my chest with a defibrillator. I got all clammy and short of breath, and it felt like my heart was going to race straight out of my chest. I knew the Holy Spirit was saying, "It's you. He's talking about you." I grabbed my bricks and mortar so fast and started building a wall. "No, God. I can't be a missionary. I can't live in Africa the rest of my life. No thanks. Not for me." My mind was filled with the stereotype that a missionary was someone who lived in a hut across the ocean, wore denim skirts, ate nothing but rice, and came to the USA to show slideshow pictures to churches every once in a while. That was not the life I had envisioned for myself. I started grabbing the back of the seat in front of me and tried as long as I could to resist. Then, before the mortar could set, I decided that I would trust God and surrender. I took a step, then another, and before I knew it, I had reached Paul. I told him I was the one he was talking about. God was calling me to missions.

Paul then introduced me to his wife, Cindy, and she explained to me that God may not ask me to go to Africa, but if He does, I have to be willing to follow Him. She helped me see that there were missions opportunities right in my hometown. I could start by being obedient there and take it one step at a time. She prayed over me and we began a relationship that, to this day, has been such a blessing to me. I came home and told my parents about the decision I made to surrender to missions. They were very supportive and encouraged me to share it publicly with my church family, which I did nervously the next Sunday. A couple of years later, I found out about a unique summer missions program in our county organized by the local Baptist association. They hired high school and college-aged students to serve in the community throughout the summer. The team of summer missionaries served many roles, like helping small churches staff their vacation Bible schools, running summer camps, and even doing events with public housing summer camps. I applied and was accepted to be a summer missionary. That program changed my life. I grew in my faith by leaps and bounds, learned great classroom and behavior management skills, became a pro at mixing Kool Aid with the proper sugar-water ratio, and met my future husband. What a win!

When the summer ended, Derek and I began dating. Contrary to popular belief, we did not date before the program ended, as that would have been breaking the very wise "no dating policy" set in place by the summer missions leaders. Derek was already in vocational ministry serving as a youth pastor when we met. After a few months of dating, we began to share our background stories with one another. I asked him how he came to be in ministry. This was the conversation that ensued:

> Derek: It was at an Exit retreat in Gatlinburg.
> Me: Oh really?! Which one?
> Derek: Exit '96
> Me: No way! Which service?
> Derek: The last night, last service. Paul said, "There is one young man here who needs to give his life to the ministry" and it was me.
> Me: I was there, and he also said, "There is one young lady here who needs to give her life to missions, and that was me!"

We were both floored to say the least! Hearing my husband tell his side of this story is also amazing because of the background information and his conversation with God during his moment of surrender. He was at the retreat with a friend's church and he was reluctant to respond to the invitation because he thought it would be better to do that at his own church back home with his family. He couldn't understand why God would be leading him to respond there where he didn't know anyone. He did go down during the invitation and speak to Paul who encouraged him in that calling. So, Derek and I walked the same aisle at the same time in surrender to God's call on our lives. We didn't notice one another during that response, and we didn't meet for another three years! God didn't want Derek to wait to surrender to the call to ministry at his home church. He wanted him to do it there in Gatlinburg, Tennessee, with his future wife in the room.

We have since reflected on that amazing story with both Paul and Cindy. They both remember it well and have even allowed us the honor of sharing the testimony at one of their more recent Exit retreats. They have invested in our marriage and our ministries over the years, and they provided the environment and opportunity for us both to break down the walls of the stereotypes in our minds of the calling to ministry and missions. The altar built that night in January of 1997 was built by dropping the bricks of a stereotype I had built in my mind of what a missionary life would be and using them to form an altar of surrender. Every time we tell that story, it seems too good to be true, but we have witnesses! Every visit to Gatlinburg is special for me, and it's not because of the taffy. It represents a place where God did amazing things in my life. Paul and Cindy are special to me. They remind me of the altar of surrender.

From God's Story

We all have stereotypes that keep us from full surrender. Jesus told a story that shattered a stereotype. In Luke 10 an expert lawyer asked Jesus a question trying to justify himself. He asked, "Who is my neighbor?" Jesus set the scene for him. The Bible says Jesus answered the question this way, "A man was going down from Jerusalem to Jericho, and he fell among robbers, who stripped him and beat him and departed, leaving him half dead. Now by chance a priest was going down that road, and when he saw him he passed by on the other side. So likewise a Levite, when he came to the place and saw him, passed by on the other side. But a Samaritan, as he journeyed, came to where he was, and when he saw him, he had compassion. He went to him and bound up his wounds, pouring on oil and wine. Then he set him on his own animal and brought him to an inn and took care of him. And the next day he took out two denarii and gave them to the innkeeper, saying, 'Take care of him, and whatever more you spend, I will repay you when I come back.'"

At the end of this story, Jesus asked the lawyer, "'Which of these three do you think proved to be a neighbor to the man who fell into the hands of the robbers?'" The lawyer accurately replied, 'The one who showed mercy to him.'" Samaritans were known to be outcasts because they were not fully Jews, and the term "Samaritan" was even used as a byword among the Jews. The stereotype was that Samaritans were lowlifes. Isn't it interesting that the lawyer can't even bring himself to say the Samaritan good guy in the story? He just says, "The one who showed mercy to him." He avoided using the specific name. This is one of the most epic linguistic flips ever made in history. In modern day, people frequently use the term "Good Samaritan" to describe someone who shows kindness to a person in need. Before Jesus, the two words "good" and "Samaritan" just didn't go together. At that time, if you called someone a Samaritan for their actions alone, it'd probably start a brawl.

An encounter with Jesus can flip a stereotype upside down. Sadly, we let stereotypes keep us from real relationships with people who are not like us because we are afraid of who we've been told they are. Too often we allow third parties to define people for us before we ever even meet them, and we just pass by on the other side of the street, never taking the chance to know them for ourselves. Don't you know many rich friendships have been formed over the years among people who should, by the world's standards, be enemies? God explains in the book of Isaiah, "For my thoughts are not your thoughts, neither are your ways my ways, declares the Lord. For as the heavens are higher than the earth, so are my ways higher than your ways and my thoughts than your thoughts." We don't get to decide what's best. We don't get to define who people are or are not. That's God's job. Our role is to be sensitive to the leading of the Holy Spirit in our lives and surrender to Him. We are responsible to show mercy to others much like we show forgiveness. Mercy and forgiveness are shown not because they have been earned by the one needing mercy or forgiveness. Rather, mercy and forgiveness are shown to them because Jesus earned it on their behalf. We don't choose who gets the mercy and who stays in the ditch. As followers of Christ, God will lead us to places we wouldn't expect with people we wouldn't expect for purposes we wouldn't expect. That's what it means for Him to be God. He is patient to guide us through difficult decisions, even when we are reluctant to surrender and follow, because He cares more deeply for us than He does a specific outcome.

From Your Story

1. How can stereotypes keep people from full surrender? Have there been stereotypes in your life that have kept you from full surrender? If so, which ones?
2. Jesus said we are being a neighbor when we show mercy to others. What are some practical ways you can show mercy to someone who, from the outside looking in, doesn't seem to deserve it?
3. How can you build an altar to remember surrendering to Jesus's authority over your life? Obedience makes a beautiful altar! How have you been or how can you be obedient to the seemingly off-script leading of the Holy Spirit?

Trading a Career for a Calling

*"There are many of us that are willing to do great things for the Lord,
but few of us are willing to do little things."*
—D.L. Moody[10]

From My Story

Circa 1995, I was a little girl standing in front of my neatly arranged rows of stuffed animals teaching them fractions using graham crackers. I had my teacher supplies stacked on my desk with plenty of red pens for grading. As far back as I can remember, I knew what I wanted to be when I grew up. In high school we had a dress up day for homecoming spirit week and we were encouraged to dress up as our dream job. Derek and I were already dating at the time, and his mom was a first-grade teacher, so I borrowed and wore her ABC earrings and hand-painted teacher sweater. My mind was set, and I was driven. During my senior year of high school, I dual enrolled and began college courses. Each semester I worked diligently, taking full loads of classes even through the summers, knocking off requirements from my course of study. In just three years, I graduated with honors from a major university with my bachelor's degree in elementary education. I was finally going to be a real teacher! I got a job out of college teaching in public school, and while there were some hard days and a few tears, I loved it! I was good at it. Things were going according to my plan.

---

[10] Moodycenter.org

Then, during my third year of teaching, my husband and I found out we were expecting our first child. The most natural path forward for my career would have been for me to take a short maternity leave and then return to teaching. It was what most people around me did. It seemed like the obvious path until it was a real decision facing us. Derek and I prayed for wisdom and direction from the Lord. During our first years of marriage, the Lord had strategically put people in our lives to challenge our view of the family as we knew it. Before getting to know two families in particular (shout out to the McClendons and the Mitchells), becoming a stay-at-home mom honestly never crossed my mind as an option. I came from a family with two working parents, so I assumed that was what everyone did and what I would do, too. Over the course of those first five years of marriage before we had children, God led me to a point where I felt a calling to stay home with our children, at least until the youngest started school. So, when the time came for our son to be born, I gave up my nice and secure teaching job and tenure position.

Those first few years of motherhood were sweet, and before I knew it, it was time to consider the education path for our kids. We felt strongly our children were a gift from God, and we were ultimately responsible for their discipleship which, in part, included their education. We wanted to be careful about the influences we allowed into their lives, especially for such large amounts of time. Derek was pastoring at a church that had a preschool program, and we considered enrolling our oldest. We prayed for God to show us what He wanted us to do. I knew the preschool was crowded, and the teachers were doing their best to care for the students, but they couldn't give them much individual attention. It seemed clear that, for that time, I was the best option for teaching my kids. Then we asked the question, "When would I not be the best option?" And just like that, for the first time, we were seriously considering homeschooling.

A friend gave me the number of a lady who directed a homeschool community near us, and I gave her a call. It was amazing. Her description of their program was like the missing edge pieces of our puzzle we had been trying to assemble in our minds. She described a God-centered classical education that didn't just teach children information, but taught children how to learn, while also giving them skills in public speaking and apologetics, among many other things. Their motto was "To know God and make Him known," and they cultivated healthy communities for like-minded families to have for support. This is what we wanted for our children. I knew from that point on, I would not be getting paid to be a teacher in a classroom full of new students each year. I let my career die, and I answered the calling to be a stay-at-home homeschool mama.

Before fully submitting to the calling on my life, I struggled when asked the question, "What do you do?" I would say, "I used to be a teacher, but now I am a stay-at-home mom." I felt the need to present myself as a capable career woman to be significant. I never planned or dreamed of being a homeschool mom. To tell you the truth, I always thought homeschool families were a little strange. But, over time, God used amazing homeschool families like the McClendons and Mitchells to show me just how significant that calling is and how incredible those kids can be. As I observed them, spent time with them, and conversed with them, bricks came down. This wall of significance through a career was faulty.

With the downed bricks, I was able to build an altar of praise for the opportunity to be my own children's teacher. While it took some time to construct, the calling gave me an altar of purpose and significance that my former career never could. God didn't waste my dreams of being a teacher. Instead, He actually refined them. I find such joy in my role as mom and teacher to our five children, and I am grateful to be able to invest in them so directly and consistently. It is unbelievably rewarding to see, year after year, the fruits of the investments I have made in each of them. There are so many outstanding benefits and precious relationships we have gained from this one decision, and looking back I see how it has been foundational in our spiritual health as a family.

From God's Story

Whom we dream of becoming and the plans we have for ourselves can often act as walls to whom God has called us to be. Consider the story of Esther. Against all odds, Esther became the queen of Persia. Hers was a real-life Cinderella story of rags to riches. Esther won the heart and favor of the king and rose to prominence. He even gave her a beautiful crown. It was a dream come true, until

Haman plotted to wipe out the Jewish people . . . Esther's people. The story is full of ironic turns and nail-biting plot twists. Ultimately, Esther had a decision to make. She could just proceed as planned with her career as the new queen, or she could submit to her calling to advocate for her people "for such a time as this." The risk was high. Not only could she lose her position, but legally, she could lose her life if she followed this calling. Esther did not take the matter lightly. She fasted and prayed and asked her closest friends in the palace to do the same, as well as all the Jews in Susa. When we are faced with life-altering decisions, we need to pull out all stops to hear from heaven. Prayer and fasting are effective multipurpose tools, useful for both the tearing down of walls and the building of altars.

After her request for prayer and fasting, Esther was resolved in her spirit. She proclaimed, "Then I will go to the king, though it is against the law, and if I perish, I perish." When you trade a self-directed career for a calling from God, the results are up to Him. Esther recognized she had no control over the king's response. All she could do was be obedient. You and I are in the same boat. All we can do is obey. The results are up to God. I can't control whether my children remain faithful or become prodigals. It's not in my power to make sure they are successful by man's standards when they grow up. My calling is to be faithful to what God leads me to do. The outcome is His business.

In Esther's story, God spared her life and used her to save His people. What if she had been content to keep the wall up and hide behind it instead of being vulnerable before the king? What would it have cost her and her people? Because of Esther's faithfulness, the lineage of the Messiah was preserved. She leveraged her influence in a way that positively impacted herself, her family and friends, future generations, and eternity.

From Your Story

1. What God-given gifts, dreams, or influence has God given you to steward for His kingdom?
2. What self-given plans or dreams are walling off your life and preventing you from fully following God's calling?
3. The Jewish people fasted and prayed on Esther's behalf. Then they created a holiday feast to remember Esther's calling and faithfulness. How can you build an altar to remember the influence God has given to you? Could you set aside a specific time to fast and pray? Could you write a poem, song, or letter to God?

7

Trading Comfort for the Great Commission

"In a culture that places great emphasis on leisure, luxury, financial gain, self-improvement, and material possessions, it will be increasingly countercultural for Christians to work diligently, live simply, give sacrificially, help constructively, and invest eternally."
—David Platt[11]

From My Story

Nine years into our marriage, Derek and I had the opportunity to attend a church planting conference for a few days, with the purpose of learning some innovative ideas to take back to our existing church. To be honest with you, I was just grateful to be on a little break from the kids at a place that fed us Chick-fil-A for lunch and kept an ample supply of good candy on our tables during sessions. The conference material was very secondary to me at the time. For the nine years leading up to that conference, Derek had served in a few different pastoral ministry roles. He would often say, "I might do a lot of different things in ministry in my life, but the two things I'm not cut out to be are a music minister or a church planter. God could use me in a variety of ways, but He just didn't gift me with those particular skills."

---

[11] Platt, *Counter Culture: Following Christ in an Anti-Christian Age*

-39-

On the second day of the conference, they divided the men and women up for lunch. I sat down at a large round table with seven other women I didn't know. One by one, they went around the table and introduced themselves. Each one had a similar story. "Hi, I'm _____. My husband and I just moved to _____. We don't know anyone there and we aren't sure how it's going to work, but we are starting a new church." Introduction after introduction felt like an arrow shooting to my heart. It was as if God was telling me, "This is going to be your story." It was clear. I started praying, "But, God, Derek says he is not cut out to be a church planter. How am I going to tell him about this?" I finally resolved to just keep it to myself. If God could tell me, He could tell him, too.

After lunch I found my seat back in the main session and grabbed a few Starbursts from the tabletop in front of me. I tried to put it out of my mind. After about an hour, I just had to say something. I just needed him to know I was ok with it if that's what God wanted from us. They had given us some Post-it Notes for the sessions. I just grabbed a pen and wrote "I'm sold" on the Post-it Note and slid it over to him. I'm not even sure how I knew he would understand what that meant. The session we were in at that moment was about website optimization, so it wasn't a hyper-spiritual moment from the platform. He received the Post-it message and looked over at me. His facial expression told me he understood. The conference lasted a few more hours, and we couldn't discuss the matter there, so we waited.

When we finally got into the car after what felt like an eternity, Derek said, "What happened in there?" I told him about the lunch and how I felt God was speaking to me. He said, "During that session I felt like God was calling us to plant a church, and I was in the middle of praying, 'God, how am I going to tell Lindsay, because for years I've said I'm not cut out to be a church planter?' Then you slid that note over to me and it was as if God was saying, 'I've already handled that part. You just need to obey.'" We both walked into that conference as "can't be church planters" and left as church planters. We knew our only options were to plant a church or be disobedient to God. It was that simple. We loved our church where we were serving, and for the first time in our marriage we were financially stable. We had a house we loved and a church family that loved our family well. We were comfortable.

What was worth giving all that up? The Great Commission was worth it. The Great Commission refers to the command from Jesus for His followers to make disciples of all nations. It was honestly a no-brainer for us to sell the house, cash out the savings and give all we had to follow God's call because it was such a clear word from the Lord. We had to revisit the altar of obedience to the Great Commission several times when reality set in and things got hard financially, emotionally, physically, and spiritually. The things we thought of as comforts were also potential idols that could have easily kept us from following the Lord. Many times we had to verbally remind ourselves that this world is not our home and eternal things are more important than temporary things, especially when planting in such a materialistic city as Miami. Thanks be to God that He walked us through those most difficult moments. He provided for us, our family, and our church in miraculous ways that we would not be able to share today had we stayed in our comfort.

From God's Story

Let's contrast two different accounts in Scripture of men who were comfortable. The first man is Job. The Bible describes Job as a "man who was blameless and upright, one who feared God and turned away from evil." It tells us he had so many possessions that he was considered "the greatest man in the east." This guy had it all: fortune, family, and faith. Satan was convinced that the only reason Job was faithful to the Lord was because of the favor and blessings given to him, so he asked permission from God to take away his fortune and family to see the real Job inside. God allowed Satan to remove Job's comforts one by one. He eventually allowed Satan to even attack Job's health. When everything was stripped away, Job had questions and raw emotions of grief and anger, but he did not abandon his faith in God. Because Job was a righteous man, he was more concerned with his right standing before God than he was his own comfort. He spent chapters seeking the Lord and looking for answers to the question "why?" but God never gave him that. All God gave him was a reassurance that God was God and Job was not. That was enough for Job. He trusted and praised God even though he had lost everything. He never, to our knowledge, would know the reason why these things happened to him.

The second man in comfort is the rich young ruler. We find his story in three of the four Gospels. Located in Matthew 19, Mark 10, and Luke 18, each account tells of a man who came to Jesus and asked Him, "Good Teacher, what must I do to inherit eternal life?" Jesus, trying to reveal a deeper truth to him, responded, "Why do you call me good? No one is good except God alone." It was a major Easter egg Jesus was dropping for him, a huge wink and elbow nudge. Only God is good. You are calling Me good. Good = God, Jesus = good, therefore Jesus = God. He follows this by strategically stating some, not all, of the Ten Commandments. He says, "You know the commandments: Do not commit adultery, Do not murder, Do not steal, Do not bear false witness, Honor your father and mother." It is interesting that He leaves out the first four commandments. These omitted commandments deal with our relationship to the Lord. Do not have any gods before me. Do not make idols out of anything. Do not take the name of the Lord God in vain. Remember the Sabbath day and keep it holy. I wonder if Jesus left those out in order to set the rich man up to be able to honestly say he had kept all the commandments Jesus listed. Or maybe He excluded those because He knew the rich man was not in a right relationship with God because he had made idols out of other things and put other gods before Him, namely the idols and gods of his possessions. I can't help but think there was a specific reason Jesus started at commandment five when He answered the rich man. Whatever the reason, the man was clueless and answered, "All these I have kept from my youth." Then, Jesus struck to the heart when He responded, "One thing you still lack. Sell all that you have and distribute to the poor, and you will have treasure in heaven; and come, follow me." The Bible tells us the man went away sad because he had great possessions. His unrighteousness was revealed by his faith in his comfort and lack of faith in Jesus. He cared more about his stuff than he did his own soul. Earthly treasures were more valuable to him than eternal treasures, and his wall of comfort kept him from experiencing the most amazing relationship possible, knowing Jesus.

Whether God takes everything from a righteous person or asks everything of an unrighteous person, the end of the story reveals each person's level of trust in God. Job trusted the Lord even when he had nothing earthy left. In contrast, the rich young ruler could not trust Jesus even though He was promising him every heavenly thing. The wall of comfort is a dangerous one. It feels so safe and nice to us, so permanent and strong. Yet, Jesus reminds us that most things in life are just hay and stubble. Only the eternal things are worth holding on to and giving your life for. Our temporary comfort on this earth is in the pile of hay and stubble, and working to fulfill the Great Commission is a great treasure we can store up in heaven for all of eternity.

From Your Story

1. What comfort do you enjoy that you can't imagine giving up? It could be a possession, a person, a position, or even a privilege.
2. Which of the commandments might Jesus highlight when speaking to you about following Him? Which ones are easier for you? Which are harder?
3. How can you build an altar to remember the unmatched value of fulfilling the Great Commission? This week, how could you invest in a person for eternity instead of a thing for a fleeting moment?

8

Trading Doubts and Anxiety for Trust in the Truth

"Doubt discovers difficulties which it never solves; it creates hesitancy, despondency, despair. Its progress is the decay of comfort, the death of peace. "Believe!" is the word which speaks life into a man, but doubt nails down his coffin."
—Charles Spurgeon[12]

From My Story

A few years into church planting in Miami, we found ourselves running at a pace impossible to maintain. We were experiencing great growth in our church, developing leaders, discipling new believers, hosting thousands of out-of-town missions volunteers, setting up and tearing down our portable church each Sunday, and doing all the things necessary to run our homeschool family and be good neighbors. Honestly, there were countless times that it just felt like there weren't enough hours in the day to get it all, or even half of it. It was exciting and fruitful work, but many times I felt like I was the top of the spiritual food chain and the entire ecosystem of Christian women's culture around me was looking to me to hold it all together. There were so many people who needed frequent counseling and discipleship, and many times it felt like there wasn't anyone sharing that burden. I didn't

---

[12] Spurgeon, *The Triumph of Faith in a Believer's Life*

feel like I had anyone aside from Derek that I could go to when I needed counseling or discipling, and his spiritual shoulders were often fatigued.

It started with a little headache. I don't normally get headaches, so I noticed it. My first thought wasn't "I should probably take some pain medicine or a nap." Instead, it was "What is that? What if I have a brain tumor? Oh my gosh, I'm dying. What if everything I've believed is a lie? How can I know that I will really have peace in my dying moments?" Y'all, it was that fast. Then, my mind wouldn't shut off. I couldn't get peace, and I felt like everything around me was closing in. I felt like I was falling into a pit of despair and doubt that had no bottom. I kept it to myself for about a day, and then I had to tell Derek.

When I shared it with him, I expected him to say, "Babe, you don't have a brain tumor. You are way overreacting here. It's ok." That's not what he said, and I'm so glad! He said, "Well, you might. I mean, you probably don't, but it does happen. That's not the serious issue here. The serious issue here is your anxiety and lack of peace." He listened, he shared, he prayed, but it didn't go away. I would love to tell you that it vanished, and all was good instantly. That's not what happened.

The next night, we went to serve at an event where Louie Giglio was speaking. Louie gave us a copy of the book he had just written called *The Comeback*. I started reading it a few days later, and in it he described a season of anxiety in his life that physically felt heavy and clouded, like a fog was covering him. This was exactly how I was feeling. He said he spent nights praying and calling out to God to free him from it, and night after night it seemed to lift just a little, until finally one day it was gone. That sounded like a good strategy to me. Through prayer and evaluation, Derek and I both came to the conclusion that my anxiety was coming from a place of spiritual depletion. I had been so busy *for* God that I neglected being *in the presence of* God. I needed to love God with my mind. Wrestling with some big doubts, I picked up the book *The Reason for God: Belief in an Age of Skepticism*. Over the course of the weeks it took to read the book, I also re-engaged in prayer, daily Scripture reading, and journaling. I could feel the fog beginning to lift, albeit just inches. The wall of doubt and anxiety was getting weak.

Then, on December 30, 2015, I walked into my bedroom to find a handwritten note on my dresser. It read:

Lindsay,

> *There have been times in our relationship when I have lived off of your faith, passion, and resolve. Whether you've ever known that or not, I don't know, but it is true. It's through such times that our Father has taught me the deeper and more eternal reasons for our marriage. Now, I open my heart even more to you and invite you to live off of my faith if you need. I can't tell you how, but I've come to know the Lord, our God, is there, and He is faithful. In probing the dark recesses of my own thoughts and questions, I've always found His light—and you will, too." From now until then, lean on me. The burden is neither heavy nor unwanted. I love you, but even more, God loves you, and He has called, saved, and sanctified you. We are not of those who shrink back and are destroyed. We are those who persevere and are saved.*

You are loved,
Derek

I couldn't even type those words just now, seven years later, without becoming a puddle. I have kept the note in a special place, and it will always be a treasure to me. My husband's loving words acted like huge beams of sunshine into my soul. They didn't burn off all of the haze, but they did penetrate the fog to reveal what was there all along. God's faithful love had surfaced. It had always been under there. He had not abandoned me, and I was not alone. My doubts and anxiety had built a wall I didn't even know was there. It took about three months for the physical weight of anxiety to subside. Through the truth spoken to me by godly authors, a loving husband who took his role as pastor and protector of his wife seriously, and God's Word, I did experience full demolition of that wall eventually. From the dust I fashioned an altar of trust in the Truth by memorizing Colossians 2:8, which says, "See to it that no one takes you captive by philosophy and empty deceit, according to human tradition, according to the elemental spirits of the world, and not according to Christ," and Hebrews 10:39, which Derek alluded to in his letter. It says, "But we are not of those who shrink back and are destroyed, but of those who have faith and preserve their souls." I can't read those verses without remembering the darkness God delivered me from. There is power in God's Word, and when we read it, we have a choice to make. Will we trust Him? In her book, *Holier Than Thou: How God's Holiness Helps Us Trust Him*, Jackie Hill Perry beautifully reasons, "If God is holy, then He can't sin. If God can't sin, then He can't sin against me. If He can't sin against me, shouldn't that make Him the most trustworthy being there is?"

From God's Story

If you were playing Bible trivia, you'd probably have no trouble filling in the person's name that goes in this blank: Doubting _____. John 20 records for us the first days after Jesus's resurrection. Jesus appeared to the disciples in a locked room. Excitedly they shared the news with Thomas, who was not with them at the time of Jesus's miraculous appearance. Because Thomas was not there to witness the miracle himself, he did not believe their testimony. He said, "Unless I see in his hands the mark of the nails, and place my finger into the mark of the nails, and place my hand into his side, I will never believe." He wanted indisputable physical evidence. There are at least three important details we need to notice from this account.

Important detail number one is that Thomas was not gathered with the other disciples when they first encountered the resurrected Jesus. The Bible does not tell us why Thomas was not with them, but I can't help but wonder if it was because he had lost all hope. I don't think he had a dentist appointment or anything. What could possibly be more important to him at a time like that than being with his brothers in the faith, comforting one another? Doubts, fears, and anxiety thrive in isolation. When we keep ourselves away from healthy fellowship with other believers, we are a huge target for the Enemy. He can steal, kill, and destroy much more effectively when we are by ourselves.

Important detail number two is that Thomas was looking for very specific scientific evidence that Jesus had, in fact, risen from the dead, and Jesus gave him very specific scientific evidence. Thomas specifically listed the nail marks in His hands and feet along with the wound in His side as necessary proofs. Jesus, being God and knowing Thomas's thoughts, entered the room miraculously as He had done before, and without Thomas having to ask Him, He offered the wounds as evidence. Sometimes our own doubts are formed because we have not been near enough to the evidence of a risen Jesus. Make no mistake, just like for Thomas, there is ample evidence for us today. We do not have to check our intelligence and logic at the door of the church. Some of the world's most brilliant minds have been dedicated to collecting solid evidence for the validity of Scripture and its claims.

Important detail number three is that Jesus came to bring peace. His first statement to the men was "Peace be with you." This was a common greeting at this time, and still is in many parts of the world. It is similar to our phrase "How are you?" Most of the time it is overlooked as meaningless banter, but in this account, it adds such rich meaning to the exchange. Jesus entered that room for a purpose. He came to bring peace. Yes, peace to them all, but specifically He appeared to give peace to Thomas. He knew that Thomas was a wreck inside, full of doubt and anxiety and lacking peace. Only Jesus could bring the peace Thomas was craving. He obliged Thomas by showing him the evidence he had asked for, then He commanded Thomas to believe, and he did! It seems at first glance like Jesus was telling Thomas how to feel, but on closer look, we see that Jesus was giving a command for Thomas to trust Him instead of his own doubts and thoughts. When Thomas confessed Jesus as Lord and God, he did so with gusto as a result of his encounter with the risen Jesus. It changed his tune from hopeless to ecstatic! As Elisabeth Elliot put it, "Faith does not eliminate questions, but faith knows where to take them." God is a big enough God to handle our doubts and questions, and He knows what to do with them. He has a way of entering our locked rooms and showing us who He really is. Once He does, our response should be ecstatic belief leading to abundant life.

From Your Story

1. What doubts or questions do you have about God that you have not addressed?
2. What happens when we are honest with God and others about our doubts?
3. How can you build an altar to remember the life-giving power of God's Word and your trust in it? What Bible verse speaks the truth that you need to write on your heart through memorization?

9

Trading the Role of Victim for Forgiveness and Healing

"Every one of us at some time has been a victim of injustice at the hands of another person. Every one of us at some time has committed an injustice against another person. People treat each other unfairly. One thing is certain: No matter how much injustice I have suffered from the hands of other people, I have never suffered the slightest injustice from the hand of God."
—RC Sproul[13]

From My Story

Over the years, I have experienced emotional nicks and scrapes from people who hurt me. Some intentionally and others unintentionally. These were small offenses that could easily be cured by an application of some proverbial Bactine spray to the heart. These minuscule violations could be effortlessly dusted off most of the time with little scarring to show for it. On the other hand, I have also experienced some deep puncture wounds to my soul that have caused me to build some substantial walls that were not so easily removed. Sadly, the deepest hurts in my life have come from within the church. While I have been hurt by family and friends in unexpected ways over my life, the most grieving hurts I have walked through have been from other church leaders.

---

[13] Sproul, *Classic Teachings on the Nature of God*

I remember as a young child, my dad, who was a pastor of a small rural church, went away on a mission trip. While he was gone, the church deacons voted to remove my dad from his position as pastor. I recall the confusion I felt when hearing the news. What had he done wrong? It basically boiled down to the deacons wanting complete control of the church. As a result, our family experienced tremendous financial strain, and from where I stood it didn't seem that any of those men cared. There was one sweet older couple in the church that loved our family deeply, and if it had not been for James and Alma, we would have literally gone hungry many days during that mess. We revisited that church years later for a homecoming service. They handed out programs that listed all the former pastors of the church throughout its history and the dates of their service time. The average tenure of a pastor in that church was eighteen months. It was sad to see so many names and dates listed. Looking back, I can see how that event gave me bricks to build a wall of distrust in church people.

Then as a young mother, a difficult situation within our church family added some bricks to my stockpile. Derek was serving as a pastor and trying to lead the church to be a missional church, but as often happens, that led to challenges. Without going into too many details, the situation was mishandled in such a way that Derek felt as though he had two options—compromise and overlook clear sin or resign. He resigned. Our family was placed under a huge financial strain. We had sacrificed financially in order to serve the church, and that had depleted all of our savings. Now, with two weeks notice, we were left without any income. To be brutally honest, we literally had no money in the bank, very little food in the house, and no idea of what we were going to do. These were people that we cared for and served alongside, when it came time to take a hard stand for truth and righteousness, many of them walked away from us. The wall got a little taller.

But God, being rich in mercy, did not let the wall stand very long. While Derek sat in the parking lot with his resignation letter in hand, praying for God to be with him as he delivered it, he got a phone call. It was from a pastor he had gone to seminary with that was looking for someone who could serve as his executive pastor. He said Derek came to his mind. This guy had no idea what had been going on in our lives. They had not connected with each other in years, but that was the moment in time that he decided to call. We believed that even if that job didn't work out, God was reminding us that He is a God who sees, knows, and provides in ways that we can't possibly expect or understand. Then, a few days after that, my grandmother (also not knowing what we were going through) decided to give each of her grandchildren some inheritance money early. The check she sent us was exactly the amount we needed to pay our bills until Derek started the new job that God *did* graciously give him. Then, on our first Sunday at that new church, the congregation rolled two shopping carts full of groceries down the aisle toward us to welcome us to their faith family. That elicited an ugly cry from me in front of all those new people. God knew we needed to be reminded of the generosity of His people after all we had just been through.

I would love to say that was the last time I was deeply hurt by church leaders, but it wasn't. We experienced deep hurt again with an unsuccessful merge, then un-merge, of our church plant with a larger church. My husband has fittingly described it this way: It's like we were kids who had spent years building this awesome, intricate one-of-a-kind LEGO creation. We took the creation to the playground, and the cool, big kid asked to hold it, but we said no several times. Then finally, the cool, big kid successfully assured us that he would be really careful with it and not let anything happen to it. He said he would even like to give us opportunities to lead other kids in making awesome LEGO creations using our designs and experience. We let him hold the creation, and before our hands were even fully released, another cool, big kid ran up to see it, bumped the first cool, big kid and because the cool, big kid holding the creation wasn't holding it carefully, he dropped it, and it shattered.

The experience of losing the identity of the church we planted felt as close to the death of a child as we could imagine. We trudged through hurt upon hurt, followed by mourning, grief, questioning, and all the emotions. We were finally granted a face-to-face meeting with "the cool big kid" in which we stated the specific ways that we believed he had sinned against us. In that meeting, he did repent and make an effort to restore what was broken. We forgave him that day and on many other days. We have forgiven him over and over again each time the temptation comes to remember with bitterness or anger. Through that season, we had dear friends, more like family, who wept with us. They carried our burden because we literally couldn't hold our own heads up. In them, we saw the best of God's people, and that gave us hope. Those people wouldn't allow us to stack the bricks any higher. They loved us too deeply, too unconditionally, for us to be able to wall them off. They spoke truth to us when we were believing lies, and they showed us that they were with us and for us in countless tangible ways.

Once these walls of being the victim of church hurt were built, it took interventions by the Holy Spirit and the body of Christ to knock them down. There were many times that I found myself asking God, "Why didn't you protect me from this?" Through these struggles, God taught me that I don't need my Savior to protect me from all the bad decisions I or others have made. I need Him to redeem and restore those bad decisions. That's more beautiful.

In my brokenness, it was not God who was unfaithful to me. On the contrary, God went above and beyond all I could ever ask or imagine to show His love and kindness to me in each of these situations. Through that love and kindness, I found strength to forgive. Only after offering genuine forgiveness did I experience healing. That forgiveness and healing built altars that looked unique in each of the situations I detailed, but they shared a common gleam. God is faithful. He knows what happens behind every closed door, and He sees into the heart of every man and woman. He does not abandon His people. He is with us always, even to the very end of the age.

From God's Story

When it comes to experiencing injustice, there is one man, other than Jesus Himself, who takes the cake. Remember Joseph? The one with the fancy coat. Joseph was the firstborn son of Jacob and Rachel. Although their relationship began like a fairy tale with her beauty bringing him to tears at his first sight of her and him working laboriously for seven years to earn her hand in marriage, things went downhill fast on the wedding night when Rachel's dad pulled a major switcharoo and gave Leah, the older sister, to Jacob instead. To make matters worse, Leah was able to conceive several sons with Jacob, but Rachel could not. After years of infertility and family strife, Joseph was finally born to Rachel. Shockingly, this didn't solve all the family problems. Their family dysfunction led to ten very jealous half-brothers plotting against Joseph.

Then Joseph had a dream that didn't sit well with his brothers. He dreamt that they would bow down to him one day, and maybe demonstrating a little immaturity, or at least poor timing, he told his brothers about the dream. That was it. They wanted him gone for good. They plotted to kill Joseph, but one brother, Ruben, convinced the brothers to just throw him into a pit. He had the secret intention of coming back to get him once their tempers died down. Before he could implement his rescue plan, the other brothers saw an opportunity to capitalize on Joseph's situation. They sold him to some slave traders. Hoping to convince their father that Joseph was killed by a wild animal, they took his fancy coat, covered it in animal blood, and presented it to their father. Don't you know they enjoyed that process a little too much? Their plan worked, the deception was successful, and Jacob was inconsolable at the loss of his favorite son.

Joseph arrived in Egypt as a slave and was sold to Potiphar, a captain of the guard for Pharaoh. Scripture tells us the Lord gave him favor and prospered everything he did, and ultimately, he was given authority over the entire house. Apparently, Joseph was a good-looking dude, and Potiphar's wife continually made advances toward him, but he was faithful to resist her each time. The final time, she trapped him, but he fled, leaving his coat behind. She used the coat to tell her story the way she wanted it to be heard. I wonder if he was thinking, "Again with the coat?!" This was the second time that his wardrobe was used against him. This time, the lies against him landed Joseph in prison. Even in prison, Joseph was faithful, and the Lord was with him and gave him success and authority.

Then, two fellow prisoners had dreams, and Joseph was able to accurately interpret them. He reported that one of them would live and be set free, but the other would die. Joseph asked the one who was destined to live to remember him when he was restored. Two. Years. Later. The Pharaoh had a dream that no one could interpret. Suddenly the freed man's memory was jogged, and he remembered his prison buddy, Joseph. Through God's power, Joseph was able to accurately interpret the Pharaoh's dream, and again, he was placed in an honored position of authority, second in command over all of Egypt. Only Pharaoh himself had more power.

Then came the amazing meant-for-Hollywood scene. A famine had struck the land and caused Joseph's brothers to travel to Egypt to seek food which Egypt had, thanks to Joseph's wise leadership and God's divine intervention in his life. The brothers bowed before Joseph himself (he refrained from saying "told ya so"), yet they did not recognize that it was him. After all, the Egyptians did dress funny, speak a different language, and wear lots of makeup. Joseph had full power to deny their request and allow them to starve. Many of us would have delighted in such an opportunity for revenge. After a couple of interactions with the brothers, Joseph finally revealed his true identity to his brothers.

Wouldn't you love to have been a fly on the wall for that moment? I cannot imagine the reaction they must have had and the fear they must have felt. Instead of using his position to seek revenge, Joseph offered his brothers full forgiveness with both his words and his actions. He assured them that they were not powerful enough to control his or anyone else's life. He said, "And now don't be worried or angry with yourselves for selling me here, because God sent me ahead of you to preserve life." Joseph saw the big picture God was painting, and He did not place any blame on his malicious brothers, Potiphar's seductive wife, or the forgetful cup bearer. He knew God had a plan, and His plan could be trusted. What healing he must have enjoyed in that truth! What freedom he experienced even while in physical chains. Joseph was confident that whatever God was up to was for his good, for the good of his family, and for the glory of God. Joseph's altar of forgiveness and healing saved his family, the nation of Israel, and the lineage of Jesus from certain destruction. God's justice in Joseph's life didn't appear to be justice at first, but Joseph had such wisdom to see past the horrible circumstances and recognize God was right in what He did.

From Your Story

1. What hurt was so deep that you find yourself still holding on to it, or coming back to it? Who do you need to forgive or forgive again? What does that look like? A phone call or text? A hand-written letter or face-to-face meeting?

2. How has your past and/or present bitterness affected you emotionally, physically, and spiritually?

3. How can you build an altar to remember the great debt for which you have been forgiven? Who can you go out of your way to serve even though they hurt you?

10

Trading Discouragement for Confidence

"Go back, Sam! I'm going to Mordor alone."
—Frodo Baggins
"Of course you are, and I'm coming with you!"
—Samwise Gamgee[14]

From My Story

Have you ever been in a crowded city, house, room, or minivan but felt completely alone? Have you ever believed the lie that no one really cares about you and no one sees you? If you have, you're not alone in feeling alone. I have been there a few memorable times in my life. About a year and a half after our un-merge with the cool, big church, Derek and I had poured everything we had emotionally, financially, spiritually, and physically into restarting our church plant with an all-new group of volunteer leaders. It was hard work. I imagine it felt about like it would if you had to get up and do hard work after having the wind knocked out of you and your legs broken out from under you. The work of planting a church is already crazy hard. When you tack on recent pain with the lack of time and resources to implement the vision and strategy we had for the church plant, we were overspent. We found ourselves asking the question "God, do You even

---

[14] Tolkien, *The Fellowship of The Ring.*

care? Do You see what we are going through over here? Why does it feel like we are the only ones fully in this?"

Sometime in late November or early December of 2017, Derek got a phone call from a friend who had financially helped our church plant several times in the past. This friend was always very generous toward our church with his resources and ideas. The phone call this time was personal. He said, "I have a strange question to ask. How are your cars?" Derek told him both our cars were running fine, and, more importantly, they were both paid for. The guy said, "Well, my wife and I both feel very strongly that the Lord has told us to buy you guys a car if there is a need." Derek thanked him, but knowing we didn't really need it, he declined the offer.

On January 1, 2018, our family was driving back to Miami from a vacation in north Georgia. It was early, around 7 a.m., and it was spitting snow. We were driving on the interstate and there was only one other vehicle in front of us. The sun wasn't even fully up yet. All of the sudden, we saw the car in front of us run off the road, over-correct, and drive straight into our lane. We collided. Thankfully no one was seriously injured, but now we were stranded. It would take an entire separate chapter to detail out how God intervened that day to provide for our family through amazing first responders. We soon got the news that the van was totaled. We began looking at used vans and trying to figure out how we could afford to add a car payment into our already airtight budget. Then, Derek got the second call. Our friend called again, only this time when Derek answered, our friend just said, "How 'bout that car now?" Derek responded with, "That would be really amazing! We have been looking at some vans about the same age as ours with about the same mileage and here is the price range we have been seeing." Our friend stopped him and said, "Forget about all that. I already know the van I want to get you. I just need to know if y'all want the hybrid version or the limited? And what color does Lindsay like?" We couldn't believe it! A few days later, this guy pulled up in our driveway with what we lovingly called a spaceship because it was so super high tech. It was beautiful! It still had the plastic wrapping on the leather seats. The kids couldn't believe it had two touch screen TVs with games installed. He handed us the keys and said, "It's yours!" His only stipulation was that he remain anonymous. Talk about biblical generosity modeled for our family. It has been a topic of conversation in that "spaceship" van many times. I would hear the kids whispering things like, "I think I know who it was. It was so-and-so wasn't it? Maybe it was this person or that." When they would ask, we would remind them that he didn't want anyone but God to get the credit for the gift, so we weren't going to work to try to figure it out. That didn't stop them from guessing and telling me they had a good idea of who it was from time to time, even now three years later.

What this couple gave us wasn't just a sleek and stylish, amazing vehicle to meet our transportation needs. They gave us the gift of hearing from God, "I see you. I know what you need before you need it, and I work on your behalf without you knowing it. You are not alone. You are not forgotten. You are Mine. You can trust Me." What confidence we gained from that reminder! It was like a second, or more like a hundredth, wind blew into our sails and we could keep going. We could keep doing the hard things until God made it clear that we were done. The author of Hebrews reminds us of this when he says, "For you had compassion on those in prison, and you joyfully accepted the plundering of your property, since you knew that you yourselves had a better possession and an abiding one. Therefore do not throw away your confidence, which has a great reward. For you have need of endurance, so that when you have done the will of God you may receive what is promised." When our focus is turned from our "better possession," that is, our hope of eternal life with Jesus, and it is turned to a lesser possession like our property or our position, we lose our confidence and thus our reward.

Discouragement makes an ugly wall, and it can isolate us from good people all around us who are trying their best to be with us and for us. We can quickly believe the lies from the Enemy that tell us we are the only ones in that fill-in-the-blank situation. The belief of that lie changes the way you look at people. It separates. When God shines His light into your heart and melts that wall of discouragement through someone in His Body of believers, it changes the way you look at people. It unites. The confidence gained from acts of generosity and encouragement from God's people is a huge faith builder. It doesn't get much clearer than this: Mark 9:40-41 tells us, "For the one who is not against us is for us. For truly, I say to you, whoever gives you a cup of water to drink because you belong to Christ will by no means lose his reward." When we are discouraged, we think everyone is against us. This is where we have to be intentional to break that lie apart and remove that wall of discouragement and build an altar of confidence in the Truth of God's Word and His people. There might be *some* who are against us, but logically, that means there are also *some* who are for us. We need to recognize the *some* that are for us and be confident in the rewards God gives to them and to us as we are faithful and obedient to Him.

From God's Story

Derek and I were not the first of God's people to believe the lie that we were all alone. One of the greatest prophets of all time also believed that same lie, and it led him to such discouragement that he ran away and hid in a cave to escape those who were against him. We are talking about a man who, at the beginning of 1 Kings 18, demonstrated such boldness as to call out 450 men who were worshiping the false god, Baal. This man was Elijah, and he challenged them to a test to see whose God (god) would show up. Then he asked for and witnessed a visible miracle from the God of heaven that included calling down literal fire and delivering what some might call irrefutable shut-up juice to all the false prophets. This is a man who heard directly from God on a regular basis, but in the middle of this miracle showdown, he revealed the seeds of this lie of discouragement taking root when he said, "I, even I only, am left a prophet of the Lord."

The very next chapter escalates to Elijah hiding in a cave, crying out to God for help because he felt like he was the only one in Israel following the Lord. God showed Elijah His power in a great wind, an earthquake, and a fire, but the Bible tells us that God's presence was not in those big, powerful things. God's presence came to Elijah through a small whisper. He was experiencing the power of God but missing the presence of God, and it was causing him to flee and fear. In that precious whisper of God, Elijah learned that there was another man of God who was ready to take his place as prophet, and seven thousand faithful Israelites who had not turned away to false gods. What a confidence booster it would be to go from believing you were the only godly one around to learning there were actually 7,001 other faithful believers nearby, ready to carry on the work of the Lord! This encounter with God gave Elijah the confidence he needed to get out of that cave and stop worrying about his enemies. He immediately went to find the new prophet, a sacrifice was made, and the new prophet immediately began assisting Elijah.

Sometimes in the middle of experiencing miracles from God, we can be blinded and begin to think there is something special about us. We can start to look around and think everyone else has "bowed to Baal and kissed him," so to speak. It is just not true! God's faithful people are all around us, and we need to be in tune with the small whisper of God instead of overly distracted by the impressive power of God. When we stop to listen to what God really has to say, we will not be so prone to believing the lies of our own hearts or those that Satan would yell at us. We will be able to live in confidence knowing that God is with us and has gone before us, and He has sent His people to be with us. Thank God that the Church is full of Samwises who would risk drowning to help their friend in a time of need.

From Your Story

1. What lies have you believed in the past that made you feel alone? Have any of those lies found their way to your heart again recently? If so, which ones?
2. What happens to us and those closest to us when we believe the lie that we are alone?
3. How can you build an altar to remember that you are not alone? What promises has God given to you in Scripture that remind you of this? (Hint: Deuteronomy 31:6, Joshua 1:5 and 1:9, 1 Kings 8:57, 1 Chronicles 28:9, Psalm 23, Psalm 27:10, Psalm 94:14, Isaiah 30:21, Matthew 28:20, John 14:18, Ephesians 2—just to name a few!)

Trading Badges of Honor
for Humility

"Much of life is building and creating supports that give us the illusion of feeling safe. Kids don't factor into that illusion."
—Samuel Rainey[15]

From My Story

Derek and I have joked for years that someone should come up with a merit badge system for parents. Parents could receive their sash at the hospital along with their first couple of badges such as the Labor and Delivery badge, the Hospital Stay badge, and the First Car Ride with a Screaming Infant until You Finally Get to the Bumpy Part of the Interstate and It Puts Him to Sleep badge. You know the one. Then, as time goes on, you could earn more badges like the Road Trip badge, the Nursed My Infant in a Store Changing Room badge, the Threw a Birthday Party badge, and the Took my Kid on a Plane badge. The list could go on and on, reaching the rare and coveted badges, like Changed a Diaper while Moving in the Line for a Ride at Disney World badge. It's a fun game we play to imagine being awarded a specific merit badge each time we survive a stressful parenting situation.

---

[15] everthinehome.com/parenting-is-hard-on-the-heart

By the time baby number five arrived, my merit badge sash was getting quite full. I had my quick and witty responses ready for the certain comments from strangers, like "You've got your hands full! Are they all yours?" I had sleep trained all five children to be soundly sleeping through the night by three months of age, and I prided myself in my disciplinarian skills over the years. It had been smooth sailing for the most part. When our fifth baby, Marshall, came along, I felt like I was an expert at the baby thing. Don't get me wrong, I knew I still had tons to learn about teen years (we were just getting started there), and managing busy schedules of multiple kids in multiple activities, but the baby thing? I was a pro! I was confident that I had it all under control. It was sure to be as smooth as Marshall's little bottom.

It didn't take long for my sash to feel worthless, like the badges were ironed on with a cheap adhesive that easily disintegrated in the south Alabama humidity. When Marshall was just three months old, I took him to the beach for the first time. I brought a beach umbrella, toys for him, and a nice light blanket for napping. While the other four kids played all day in the shallow water, Marshall nursed a little, played a little, but spent most of the time laying under the beach umbrella napping face up. He was too young to wear sunscreen, so I was very careful to keep him in the shade of the umbrella. At the end of our beach day, when I got him to the car, I noticed his face was really red. I thought he might just be a little over heated, so I turned the air on full blast. When we got home, it was clear that he was not just hot, he was severely burned. His face had begun to blister within the hour it took for us to drive home. I felt like such a failure. I quickly called the doctor, and she walked me through a few options for treatment. It was a long, painful week for Marshall and for me. He was in so much pain that he could only nurse in one very specific position that left me feeling like a very tired and sore contortionist wannabe. His face scabbed over, and after about seven days, finally, the sores just washed away in his bath. I literally cried in joy and thought about how happy the blind man must have been to see the scales wash from his eyes when Jesus healed him. The skin left behind looked so new and smooth. It was beautiful!

Then, a few months later, the kids and I were packing up to leave for a full day at our homeschool co-op. I had wheeled Marshall out in his car seat-stroller travel system, and I turned to answer a question our new cleaning lady was asking me, but I didn't put the brakes on the stroller. When I turned back around, his stroller was gone. It didn't immediately hit me. I thought my older son had put him and his car seat in its base and loaded up the stroller in the back of our van as he often would do. I walked around the van saying, "Where's Marshall?" I even looked back in through the side door to see if I had actually forgotten to wheel him outside in all the commotion. Then, to my horror, I saw my youngest daughter's sippy cup in our neighbor's grass. I knew it had been sitting in the cup holder of Marshall's stroller. I started running down our incredibly steep driveway looking for his stroller. Finally, I saw it. It was laying on its side facing away from me in the grass of our neighbor's yard ACROSS THE (BUSY) STREET. I ran as hard as my legs could take me, terrified of how I would find him when I got to him. Holding my breath, I looked over the canopy of the car seat which was still snapped into the stroller. By God's amazing grace, he was laughing and unharmed. I hoisted his stroller back to the upright position and pushed it halfway up our driveway, which at this point felt like Mt. Everest. My other four kids came running, and I just became jello. We huddled around his stroller and prayed with tears, thanking God for His protection over Marshall. I felt like such a failure. Again. On the car ride to our co-op, my mind filled with endless scenarios that could have happened. I was shaking in fear and shame. I wanted to just tuck it away as a close call and forget about it. I didn't. First, I called my husband and told him what happened. He was calm and reassuring, overwhelmingly gracious toward me, and grateful to God for His protection. Next, when I got to our co-op, I saw another mom who I greatly respect, and I fought the urge to answer her "How are you today?" with a phony "Fine." Instead, I wept in front of her and told her what I had done. She hugged me and prayed with me, thanking God with me for His protection over Marshall and asking Him to help me fight the battle in my mind with my guilt.

A little over a year after that, I had to make my first call to Poison Control as a mother. The kids and I were on the last day of a COVID quarantine, and I needed to give a pitch for the small group I would begin leading the next week at church. Hoping to persuade some ladies to sign up, I did a quick Zoom call in to church and shared the details of my upcoming class about motherhood. I thought the kids were all upstairs in the playroom during the ten-minute call, but when I went upstairs, Marshall was not there. When I called for him, he responded with, "Yes!" and the sound was coming from my bathroom. I walked in to find him standing there surrounded by pills. He had opened four childproof pill bottles and had some white residue on his lips and tongue. My heart sank, and my mind raced with all the panicked questions, "What has he ingested? How much? What's going to happen to him now?" I felt like such a failure. Again, again. I called Derek, who was at church where I had just Zoomed, and told him what happened. He confirmed that I needed to call Poison Control immediately, and he rushed home. The Poison Control nurse was amazingly calm and reassured me that none of the medications I listed were life-threatening for him. She gave me instructions on what to do and how to monitor him over the next few hours, and praise God, he was just fine. Two of our pastors' wives came right over, hugged me tight, cried with me, and just sat with me. About a week later, when my heart had finally stopped racing from the near-tragic incident, I wrote an article detailing the event and the lesson God taught me in it.

In each of these three instances, I wanted to build a wall of "No one has to know I messed up. No one has to see my mothering mistakes. I can pretend I've got it all well-balanced and running smoothly." It would have been much easier on my pride to keep quiet about these things. My wall would have looked so impressive decorated with the parenting merit badges on the outside. I could have hidden behind it so naturally. Instead, the Holy Spirit convicted me and led me to be vulnerable and speak up to those close to me, and even in these specific instances, publicly. Had I not done that, I would have blockaded myself from intimacy with my husband, my friends, my fellow pastors' wives, and those I lead. I would have been consumed with my guilt (some real, some false) and been left to grieve alone. I would have isolated myself from the wisdom of those who loved and cared for me most. Most importantly, I would have wrongly continued thinking I was the one in control of my children's well-being, and that *I* was why they were the way they were—good or bad.

From God's Story

We often don't associate humility with strength. In fact, when we think about strength, usually what comes to mind is physical strength. Interestingly, the guy in the Bible most famous for his physical strength was greatly lacking in humility. Samson was born to two godly parents who were literally taught their parenting skills face-to-face by angels. Talk about a merit badge! They made amazing vows that included Samson's mom avoiding certain things during her pregnancy which would set Samson apart as a Nazarite and continued with Samson himself avoiding those things as well. The Bible says Samson grew, the Lord blessed him, and the Spirit of the Lord began to stir in him. The Spirit of the Lord empowered him to have such strength that he was able to kill a lion with only his hands.

Immediately after this victory, Samson broke one of his Nazarite vows, the vow not to touch any unclean animal. He kept it hidden from his parents, likely because he didn't want to be shamed by them. A few bricks of his wall of badges were up. Then, over time, broken vow by broken vow, Samson built a wall so tall that to bring it down was going to cost him his life. Samson began to forget Who was the real Source of his strength. His arrogance led him to his weakest moment. Blinded from the removal of his eyes by the Philistines and weakened by his rebellion against God, Samson stood between two supporting pillars of a building as entertainment for his enemies. He had reached his rock-bottom. Humiliation. In his degradation, he chose not to look to himself for strength. Rather, he recognized God as the true Source of his strength and called out to Him for help. His plea was honorable and humble and brought glory to God. The Lord did give him strength one last time and used him to destroy more of his enemies in that one moment than he had in his entire life combined, but it took his life as well.

Samson was comfortable being the strong guy. He knew how to fight and kill. His strength was his source of identity rather than the Source of his identity being his strength. If Samson had remained humble and faithful to the Lord, his story would have been very different. How much stronger could he have been had he kept the gifts of God in their rightful place? How many more enemies could have been defeated? Strength is a wonderful gift, but it's a lousy god. When the gifts God has given us become greater in our eyes than Him or lessen our dependence on Him as our Life Source, those gifts are no longer gifts. They have become idols. Idols are as useless as a sash full of ironed-on merit badges.

From Your Story

1. In what area of your life do you see the danger of pride creeping in and keeping you from full humility and a healthy dependence on God?

2. What good gifts has God given to you that can easily become idols in your heart? How can you shift your focus away from the gift (idol) and toward the Giver?

3. How can you build an altar to remember the gracious protection of God from the what-ifs and acknowledge Him as the Giver of good gifts? Is there a story you've never shared (or maybe you've embellished it to paint yourself in a better light) that you need to intentionally share with someone who might need to see your humility displayed?

Trading Happily Ever After for Joy Now and Forever

"But like all dreams, I'm afraid this won't last forever."
—Fairy Godmother[16]

From My Story

My favorite Disney princess is Cinderella. I love the story of peasant to princess and good winning over evil. Everything about Cinderella. Her beautiful singing, her ability to talk to animals, her gorgeous dress, and her mic-drop moment when she pulls out the other glass slipper after the first one was broken captivate me. Our family has enjoyed several trips to Disney World. There is nothing quite like a good kiss with my own Prince Charming in front of the castle at the happiest place on earth. In April of 2021, our family was enjoying one of those magical trips. Even in the middle of a worldwide pandemic, we had a wonderful visit and were able to check off almost all of our must-do experiences. Because of the park reservation system put in place during COVID, we were not able to go to Epcot on the last day of our trip as originally planned. We debated staying at the condo the extra day, but finally decided just to go on home and give ourselves some down time to unpack and relax on Saturday before another busy Sunday. About twenty minutes from home Derek started experiencing some abdominal pain. Throughout the night, the pain only worsened,

---

[16] *Cinderella*, 1950

so he went to the urgent care first thing Saturday morning. He called me from the doctor's office to tell me they suspected appendicitis, but they wanted him to go across the street to the hospital for a CT scan to confirm. I called in a babysitter and went to meet him at the hospital.

By the time I reached the hospital, Derek was in excruciating pain. After a long wait, they called him back for the scan. Then, they came back and said they wanted to do the scan again because they couldn't see everything clearly. They told us if appendicitis was confirmed, they would take him straight to surgery. After the second scan, the tech said the urgent care office would call us with the results. When the doctor called, she said, "We want you to come back over to our office to discuss the results and his options." That was weird. Options? So, we drove back across the street to the urgent care office. The doctor explained that Derek did appear to have an inflamed appendix, but while doing the scan they discovered a tumor on his kidney. She explained that it was likely renal cell carcinoma. From that point it was a whirlwind. We went to the hospital, where Derek met one doctor for his appendicitis and another for the kidney tumor. They consulted and agreed that Derek needed to get the appendix taken care of first, then the tumor. The urologist explained to us that the cancer they found was a silent kind, and without the appendicitis, it would have gone unnoticed until it was too late. Suddenly, my strong husband was weak, and my heart was breaking over the thought of losing him, and there wasn't anything he or I could do about it. They operated on him the next day and removed his appendix. During the surgery the doctor also found and removed a tissue band restricting his intestines. He healed for six weeks, then was operated on again to remove the tumor. The operation went very well, and all the cancer was successfully removed. After that surgery, he was unable to drive for three weeks, and unable to lift anything heavier than a half-gallon of milk for eight weeks.

During the diagnosis, treatment, and recovery process, I found myself wanting to plug the holes now showing in the wall I had built since I was a kid. In my mind, I knew the way things were supposed to be: fall in love, get married, live happily ever after. That was how it was supposed to work. Up until this point, I could basically describe my life that way. My marriage had felt as close to a fairy tale as possible without talking mice and a magic wand. I found myself wanting to hide my raw emotions from Derek because I knew it would be hard for him since there would be nothing he could do to fix it. Of course, I struggled with the fear of losing him, but that wasn't my biggest fear. I broke down emotionally several times in fear that if I did lose him, I might not be able to remember enough of him. I was terrified that I would forget what it felt like to be around him, to be held by him, to be kissed by him. My mind kept fixating on things, like "What if I don't remember what it feels like to be safely tucked under his arm while we relax on the couch?" or "What if I forget what he smells like?" Since Alzheimer's disease runs in my family, that fear has tucked itself in my mind from time to time, but it didn't surface very often, mainly because I assumed it would come when I was much, much older, and I figured I would enjoy many years of life with my full memory. I had never honestly faced the thought of going so many years without Derek. It scared me. There were moments with him that I couldn't focus on the present joy because all I could think was "What if I lose him soon, and I can't remember this very moment?" I sometimes even found myself wishing he wasn't such an amazing husband, father, and friend. "That would make it easier if I had to lose him," I would think. I often worked overtime to hide the warm, steady tears at night. The wall of Happily Ever After was keeping me from true joy and peace in the now.

After several weeks of this, I decided to break down the wall. I made the decision to give up the empty idea of Happily Ever After and embrace intimacy with my husband. I shared with him about my fear of forgetting all the little things if I were to lose him. He hugged me and let me cry. Then Derek pointed me to the Truth of the Gospel. He lovingly told me that Jesus is enough for me. He is better than our marriage. He is better than my memories. He encouraged me to trust that Jesus is enough for me now and will be enough for me no matter what the future holds. He showed me how my fear of what is not was robbing me of my joy of what is and what is to come. We prayed together, and he regularly checked on me in my process to trust the Lord through the struggle. When I look at the words now in black and white, it is so clear to see that these lies I was believing were straight from the Enemy. How ridiculous is it that I would wish for a lousy husband just so the thought of losing him didn't have to be so painful? I was literally telling God, "The good gifts you have given to me are not appreciated or wanted because I don't want to have to ever give them up." I was ignoring the eternal joy that I have gained through our marriage and the kingdom impact our relationship has made on both of us, our children, and the many other families we have been able to disciple. Satan would love to rob me of the joy I have been given through my marriage. I am so grateful that God did not allow that to happen in this story. I am grateful for His good gifts and submit to His authority to say how long those gifts are to be enjoyed here on Earth.

After Derek's surgery, the prognosis was very good. He will have to go for scans annually for several years to make sure it doesn't come back, and that's it. No chemo or radiation was necessary. Another good gift from the Lord, and we are so grateful! We never thought we would thank God for appendicitis, but here we are. Had it not been for his abdominal pain from the blockage and appendicitis, we never would have found the cancer growing in him. That cancer gave me the courage to break down a faulty wall and build a deeper intimacy with my husband and my God that will go with me into eternity. There's no threat of a strike at midnight ending that!

From God's Story

What does the Bible say about holding on to life as we want it? Jesus addressed this issue directly several times. My favorite is found in Matthew 16 when He says, "If anyone would come after me, let him deny himself and take up his cross and follow me. For whoever would save his life will lose it, but whoever loses his life for my sake will find it. For what will it profit a man if he gains the whole world and forfeits his soul? Or what shall a man give in return for his soul?" To come after Jesus means denial of yourself. This is to say "no" to our ideas, our dreams, our plans. To say "no" to ourselves will lead us to take up our cross. To take up our cross will lead us to follow Jesus. To follow Jesus is to arrive at the same destination as He does. To arrive at the same destination as Jesus means to be in His presence where there is fullness of joy! Now *that* sounds like a happy ending, which is actually not an ending at all.

This teaching is not just something Jesus randomly said. In context, this comes just after Jesus foretold His own death. The Bible says, "From that time Jesus began to show his disciples that he must go to Jerusalem and suffer many things from the elders and chief priests and scribes, and be killed, and on the third day be raised." He was giving them the details of His own suffering and death. Good ol' Peter didn't want it to be true. It didn't fit his preconceived ideas about who the Messiah should be. He was looking for a Victor. He wanted his Happily Ever After with Jesus leading the way. How could that happen if He was killed?! Jesus didn't take Peter's objection lightly. When Peter said, "Far be it from you, Lord! This shall never happen to you." Jesus quickly responded, "Get behind me, Satan! You are a hindrance to me. For you are not setting your mind on the things of God, but on the things of man." Our storybook endings are often a result of having our minds set on the things of man rather than the things of God.

We would write it differently. Of course we would. We aren't God. If we held the pen, we would only include the things that bring us glory and pleasure. We would write a story of selfishness, making sure no trouble, pain, or loss crept into any of the pages. Jesus teaches us that His plan for life is more abundant than any autobiography we could muster. He offers abundant life both now and forever, but we have to first lay down our version of life. What does it look like to lay down our life? For some, it looks like literally laying down the very breath in their lungs as a martyr. For others, it looks like being willing, at any moment, to give up the things that are most precious to them if the Lord asks for it, or as in some cases, being joyful to release it if God takes it from them. There is abundant joy and freedom when we can come to a place where we can honestly say of any loss, "Because God has allowed this to happen in my life, I can trust that it is for my good and His glory. Somehow, 10,000 years from now, I will be thanking God for it. I trust Him." When we move beyond mere acceptance of our daily crosses to fully embracing them with gratitude, we find life. When we genuinely thank God for even our sorrows, then we have taken up our cross and followed Jesus. The stuff, the status, and even the memories are not so valuable that they are worth trading for our soul. There are so many shadows of life, things the Bible describes as hay and stubble, that we spend our time trying to hold, all the while missing out on the real life and joy now and forever that God offers to us.

From Your Story

1. What do you have that you fear losing?
2. Pastor John Piper wrote, "Life is not a straight line leading from one blessing to the next and then finally to heaven. Life is a winding and troubled road. Switchback after switchback. And the point of biblical stories like Joseph and Job and Esther and Ruth is to help us feel in our bones (not just know in our heads) that God is for us in all these strange turns. God is not just showing up after the trouble and cleaning it up. He is plotting the course and managing the troubles with far-reaching purposes for our good and for the glory of Jesus Christ." How have you found this to be true in your own life?
3. How can you build an altar to remember that your life is in God's good and sovereign hands? What is a loss that you have not been able to thank God for? Even if you haven't seen the way He has or is turning it for good, what bigger truths do you know about God that currently lead you to trust Him and His outcome rather than your own

13

Keeping Walls Down, Altars Up, and Boundaries Clear

"I want to stay in the habit of 'glancing' at my problems and 'gazing' at my Lord."
—Joni Eareckson Tada[17]

I recently had the opportunity to visit Israel for the first time. As one of our guides said, "In America you count time by hundreds of years. Here we count by thousands." At almost every site we visited, we saw remains from multiple time periods stacked on top of one another. One group would build a wall or fortress, another would come and conquer them, breaking down much of the wall or fortress, then rebuilding on what remained. This pattern happened several times over the course of thousands of years, leaving walls with layers that marked each civilizations' turn there. You have read some of my personal wall stories along with various passages of Scripture paired with each one, and you've asked and answered questions of reflection about your own story. Maybe you have already started removing some of your own walls and building some meaningful altars as a sign of remembrance. If you are reading this, you are still living your life. The tricky part is, when life is still being lived on this side of heaven, sin is still very present, and we are called to crucify it daily. I wish I could tell you that this book contains the entirety of my walls, they are all cleaned up, and

[17] Joniandfriends.org

there's nothing but altars around my heart as far as the eye can see. That would not be the truth. Just like those walls in Israel, our walls have layers on top of layers. I haven't always done a great job of cleaning up each wall completely in order to begin a new season with a smooth and clean surface. Additionally, I have to be intentional about revisiting the altars I've built, and oftentimes when I do I discover they are dusty, empty, and in desperate need of a good pressure cleaning for lack of frequent use. I find myself going through difficult situations that reveal new walls I had not known were there. Sometimes these events shed light on old sections of my walls that I thought had already been carted out years prior. It is a never-ending task to fight the temptation to withdraw from others in an unhealthy way. On the other hand, it is a joy for all eternity to give glory to God and spend time in communion with Him and His people. We cannot let the unhealthy civilizations of our flesh build up and stick around for so long that they eventually draw in gawking tourists. We must daily choose to maintain what's healthy and life-giving and remove what's not.

Is it healthy and life-giving to remove *all* separation from others? Should I be an open book and share any and all known information to any and all people I come in contact with? Should I go ahead and include my social security number and bank account information in this chapter for anyone to read? Should I tell the grocery delivery lady my deepest fears as she hands me the bananas and apples? Clearly not. Some separation is healthy. In Ecclesiastes 3:7, Scripture teaches us that there is a time to speak and a time to be silent. The key is this, we must be willing to share anything and everything the Holy Spirit leads us to share at any time with anyone, while relying on prayer and godly wisdom to discern unwise transparency or vulnerability. We are not necessarily an open book, but we aren't a locked diary either. God doesn't ask us to share everything every time with everyone, but you'd better believe He does ask us to share some things we would rather not at times we would not prefer with people we don't yet fully trust (or sometimes even know!).

Property and national boundaries are important for clarifying what belongs to whom and who has authority over what. They provide proper balance and order so that neighbors can interact peaceably with one another, avoiding even accidental encroachment or wrongful use of land. Boundaries elicit partnerships and allies, and they can give you that "finally, I'm home!" feeling. Unlike walls, boundaries are made of air. They are abstract, set by an authority, and able to be adjusted by that authority. Almost all of my kids have had that ah-ha moment when on a road trip. Maybe your kids have experienced it, too. You're driving along, and you see a new welcome sign for a neighboring state. Then the kid asks, "Where is the line, Mommy?" They have seen the lines on the map, but it's not there in real life. So it is with emotional boundaries. The problem is, we often think of ourselves as the rightful authority who sets our emotional boundaries. We think we own the land of our heart and soul, and we foolishly believe it's our decision who we let in and who we keep out. Look a little more carefully at that deed. We can often be deceived into thinking our name is on it, and as a result, we think we have the ultimate authority and control over where the boundaries are. Maybe we even think of it like God has cosigned with us on the loan, but we are the primary owners. The Bible clearly shows us that God has the full authority over everyone. Psalm 135:6 says, "Whatever the Lord pleases, he does, in heaven and on earth, in the seas and all deeps." That's pretty much everywhere, in case you didn't catch it. Even when we think we are in charge, we're not. We aren't even eligible for a cosign. God gets to decide our boundaries, not us.

An emotionally and spiritually mature person has healthy boundaries in relationships. Take Jesus, for example. He taught and ministered to the crowds, He lived in community with the twelve, and He deeply and intimately invested in the three. In his book *Emotionally Healthy Spirituality*, Peter Scazzero says, "Christian spirituality, without an integration of emotional health, can be deadly—to yourself, your relationship with God, and the people around you." Not even Jesus emotionally invested on the same level with every person He came in contact with. He didn't carry every person's emotional load *when* they wanted Him to *how* they wanted Him to. In fact, He often retreated so He could better invest in the few that He knew would effectively multiply His mission. However, there were a few special times that He did feel led to share more deeply with another person who was not a disciple. It was without exception for a greater purpose: to glorify God. To be human is to have limited time, limited resources, and limited emotional and physical energy. When we choose to say "yes" to one person, we are logically saying "no" to others. Just as God instructs us to be wise stewards of our financial resources, weighing out the costs and returns for those investments, we must also wisely steward our time and emotional and physical resources. In Matthew 10:14, Jesus says, "And if anyone will not receive you or listen to your words, shake off the dust from your feet when you leave that house or town." He is telling us that not everyone is a wise investment for our emotional resources, and that's ok.

So, for the glory of God, let us do everything we can to live at peace with one another. When we have opportunities to deepen relationships, let's take them. When we are tempted to build and maintain walls of "Bless your heart. Y'all come back real soon," or of constant suspicion and mistrust, let's follow the guidance of the Holy Spirit rather than our own cultural norms. As the Lord works and moves in our hearts as well as around us in circumstances, let us acknowledge His work and frequently build altars of remembrance. And let us submit to the Lord as our ultimate authority and creator and maintainer of our boundaries. Let's keep our walls down, our altars up, and boundaries clear. It really is a prime deal, trading walls for altars.

Made in United States
Orlando, FL
10 August 2022